"Having already opened the eyes of the body of Christ to its treasury of devotional poetry in *The Soul in Paraphrase*, Leland Ryken now widens our vision to take in the depth and breadth of two millennia of devotional prose. Running the gamut from the giants of the genre (Augustine, John Donne, Jonathan Edwards, Martin Luther, Brother Lawrence, Blaise Pascal, Julian of Norwich, Bernard of Clairvaux) to writers we do not usually identify with devotional writing (Florence Nightingale, Samuel Taylor Coleridge, George MacDonald, Jane Austen, George Washington Carver), *The Heart in Pilgrimage* conducts its readers on a spiritual journey that is well worth taking."

Louis Markos, Professor in English and Scholar in Residence, Houston Baptist University; author, *The Myth Made Fact: Reading Greek and Roman Mythology through Christian Eyes*

"This collection gives the gift of informed access to a great mixed chorus of voices with often surprising words that prick our imaginations and our hearts of faith. Even as we read and celebrate a glorious heritage of devotional expression, we are drawn ultimately to worship the glorious Lord God of the Scriptures who created us human beings and redeemed us through his Son."

Kathleen B. Nielson, author; speaker

"This is an edifying volume of diverse devotional texts skillfully excerpted and each followed by a brief overview. The texts span centuries, and Ryken's editing makes them very accessible. The texts are marked by artful and clear expression, and all invite readers to open their hearts to God and experience his grace."

James C. Wilhoit, Professor of Christian Education Emeritus, Wheaton College

"Whenever I am asked to recommend a volume that combines literary study with sound Christian teaching, I recommend Leland Ryken. His new collection of rich devotional literature will move to the top of my list of recommended works. *The Heart in Pilgrimage* is a treasury of wisdom and beauty to which readers will return again and again."

Karen Swallow Prior, author, *On Reading Well: Finding the Good Life through Great Books*

"Like cool water to a parched throat, Leland Ryken has produced a soul-quenching gift with this collection of devotionals. Filled with beautiful writing devoted to an even more beautiful subject, *The Heart in Pilgrimage* delivers the truths of the Christian faith through masterful expression, promising to awaken fresh affections for the Lord among believers of every stripe."

Collin Huber, Senior Editor, Fathom Magazine

THE HEART IN
PILGRIMAGE

THE HEART IN PILGRIMAGE

A Treasury of Classic Devotionals on the Christian Life

Leland Ryken, editor

WHEATON, ILLINOIS

The Heart in Pilgrimage

Copyright © 2022 by Leland Ryken

Published by Crossway
    1300 Crescent Street
    Wheaton, Illinois 60187

Cover design: Jordan Singer

First printing 2022

Printed in China

Unless otherwise indicated, Scripture quotations in the devotional commentary by Leland Ryken are from the ESV® Bible (The Holy Bible, English Standard Version®), copyright © 2001 by Crossway, a publishing ministry of Good News Publishers. Used by permission. All rights reserved. The ESV text may not be quoted in any publication made available to the public by a Creative Commons license. The ESV may not be translated into any other language.

Scripture quotations marked KJV are from the King James Version of the Bible. Public domain.

Scripture quotations marked RSV are from the Revised Standard Version of the Bible, copyright © 1946, 1952, and 1971 the Division of Christian Education of the National Council of the Churches of Christ in the United States of America. Used by permission. All rights reserved.

All emphases in Scripture quotations have been added by the author.

Scripture quotations in reprinted devotional passages have been left in their original form and translation.

Hardcover ISBN: 978-1-4335-7779-6
Epub ISBN: 978-1-4335-7782-6
PDF ISBN: 978-1-4335-7780-2
Mobipocket ISBN: 978-1-4335-7781-9

Library of Congress Cataloging-in-Publication Data

Names: Ryken, Leland, editor.
Title: The Heart in Pilgrimage: A Treasury of Classic Devotionals on the Christian Life / Leland Ryken, editor.
Description: Wheaton, Illinois : Crossway, [2022] | Includes bibliographical references and index.
Identifiers: LCCN 2021055063 (print) | LCCN 2021055064 (ebook) | ISBN 9781433577796 (hardcover) | ISBN 9781433577802 (pdf) | ISBN 9781433577819 (mobipocket) | ISBN 9781433577826 (epub)
Subjects: LCSH: Devotional literature. | Spiritual life—Christianity. | Christian life. | Theology.
Classification: LCC BV4801 .F54 2022 (print) | LCC BV4801 (ebook) | DDC 242/.2—dc23/eng/20220128
LC record available at https://lccn.loc.gov/2021055063
LC ebook record available at https://lccn.loc.gov/2021055064

Crossway is a publishing ministry of Good News Publishers.

RRDS   31   30   29   28   27   26   25   24   23   22
15   14   13   12   11   10   9   8   7   6   5   4   3   2   1

This book is dedicated to all Crossway personnel
who have blessed me through the years
with their competence and dedication to Christian publishing.

Contents

Editor's Introduction

This book is an anthology of prose devotional classics. Each passage is accompanied by an explication of a devotional text. This book was conceived and composed as a companion volume to *The Soul in Paraphrase: A Treasury of Classic Devotional Poems* (Crossway, 2018). In this introduction, I hope to delineate the nature and purpose of this book, explain the criteria by which the passages were selected, provide an anatomy of types or genres under the umbrella of prose devotional, and explore the techniques by which a prose devotional can rise above the conventional devotional to attain the status of a classic.

The Nature and Purpose of This Book

This book is a collection of fifty devotionals composed by forty-six authors over a span of seventeen centuries. The selections are evangelical in viewpoint. Under that umbrella, they encompass a wide range of denominations and traditions. The arrangement of these selections is neither chronological nor topical, but is instead designed to achieve a pleasing variety and spontaneity. Monotony and predictability are a besetting weakness of conventional anthologies of devotionals, and as editor of this volume I worked hard to counteract this syndrome.

What is a devotional? The defining traits of a prose devotional are the same as those of a devotional poem, except that the medium is prose rather than poetry. A devotional is definable by its subject matter first of all. It takes specifically religious and spiritual experience for its subject. Examples are the person and works of God, personal salvation and sanctification, trust in God, relating to God day by day, meditations on specific Christian doctrines, and godly living.

A second avenue toward defining the devotional genre is by its effect on a reader. A devotional is not primarily an exposition of doctrine, and it does not appeal to our intellect the way a theology book or sermon does. Instead it is *affective* in its operation, appealing to our emotions and heart more than our minds. The purpose of a devotional is not to inform or educate but to bend the soul toward God and persuade a reader to embrace godliness in daily life. A devotional also provides paths by which to attain such godliness.

Because of these considerations, I have drawn passages very sparingly from sermons, and when I have taken passages from sermons, I have chosen material that meets the criteria of devotional writing as defined earlier. A direct statement of doctrinal truth, or the exposition of a specific Bible passage, belongs to the realm of expositional writing rather than devotional writing, which is designed to move us and awaken the motion of our soul toward God.

The purpose of this anthology is first of all to provide a rich devotional experience. Because the selections attain the status of a classic through superior technique and beauty of form, a secondary goal is literary enjoyment and artistic enrichment. I have also envisioned an educational purpose to my enterprise in the sense that I have aimed to acquaint my readers with the canon of famous devotional works of the Christian tradition.

Each selection is accompanied by what literary scholars call an explication. An explication is an explanation and analysis of a text, especially in the form of close reading. The twofold purpose of such commentary is to enhance a reader's understanding and enjoyment of a text. In composing my explications, I have undertaken to show what makes each selection great, and to outline avenues toward appreciation and spiritual application. In this endeavor, I have viewed myself as a tour guide, pointing things out and saying, "Look." The range of what I have put into my explications is broad and varied, but everything answers to my goal of putting my readers in possession of the text and enhancing their experience of it. The best way to combine the devotional passages with the explications is first to read the devotional, then read my explication as a way of reaching a fuller understanding and enjoyment of what has just been read, and then read the devotional a second time, using the tips from my explication as a lens through which to view the passage.

Criteria for Selection of Passages

The primary criterion by which I selected the entries in this anthology was that a passage needed to provide an uplifting devotional experience. A classic devotional needs to meet a spiritual criterion first of all. But what raises a devotional above ordinary expository prose? As an entry point to answering that question, we can listen to Charles Spurgeon. The fountainhead from which the modern daily devotional book flows is Spurgeon's *Morning and Evening*. Spurgeon himself tells us how it all started. As he looked at the available devotional guides, he was dismayed by their dullness, predictability, monotony, and lack of fresh insight and expression.

What, then, are the traits that raise a devotional above such limitations? It is not superior truthfulness that makes the difference. Conventional expository devotionals couched in everyday prose are not deficient in their religious truth. They are deficient at the level of form and expression. The following anatomy of how a devotional rises above the level of the mundane will be abundantly illustrated by the selections in this anthology.

First, a classic devotional possesses excellence of literary form and expression. More often than not, this literary and rhetorical excellence is stylistic in nature, tending toward eloquence and polish. These qualities should not be dismissed as "only the form" of a devotional passage, or a kind of decoration. The verbal beauty and rhetorical skill are part of the total effect of a passage. Truth stands out with greater clarity and impact for being expressed in masterful form, as the Bible itself illustrates. Masterful expression also stays in one's memory instead of being quickly forgotten.

But literary polish is not the only avenue toward attaining distinctiveness. Some of the selections in this anthology are at the opposite end of the stylistic continuum from elegance. They achieve distinctiveness by their simplicity or everyday realism or quaintness or sheer unusualness. A classic needs to overcome the cliché effect of the overly familiar and expected, and there are many ways to achieve it. Readers of this anthology will be pleased to see how many avenues exist toward the attainment of freshness and vigor.

There is another trait that most of the entries in this anthology possess, and that is an element of surprise or paradox. More often than not, there is something present in a classic devotional that challenges a conventional outlook—some element of dissonance that requires analysis and perhaps adjustment in our thinking. The commentary that I have provided in my explications will make this aspect plain.

Two remaining criteria are complementary to each other. As already stated, one of my goals is to acquaint my readers with the familiar canon of classic devotional works. Wherever possible, I have titled the selections in such a way as to retain the title of an author's signature work—the book or shorter piece with which the author is linked in our minds. Additionally, a few of the selections are present by virtue of their importance in Christian history—selections such as Martin Luther's preface to his commentary on Galatians and Governor Bradford's exhortation to the Pilgrims who survived their first winter (during which half of the arriving party died).

But although familiarity was thus one criterion, I have also been innovative. I hope that in looking at the table of contents of this anthology my readers will be surprised at some of the authors and texts that made the cut. I deliberately tapped unexpected sources for some of my entries—sources such as the burial service from the Prayer Book, the opening questions and answers of famous catechisms, the bidding prayer from Lessons and Carols, last wills and testaments, and the prefaces to two famous English Bibles.

Genres of Devotional Writing

My readers will navigate this anthology more smoothly if they are aware of how many different genres are represented in devotional writing. My purpose here is to provide an anatomy of these genres.

Just as lyric poems fall into the two categories of reflective and affective or emotional, so do prose devotionals. Most of the devotionals in this anthology are reflective pieces. A reflection does not follow the standard pattern of expository writing, where a thesis is presented and then supported with data. A reflection is a process of thinking on a subject that has been introduced. Usually the author or speaker in the passage is foregrounded in such a way that we are aware of a person thinking through an issue or experience and sharing a sequence of thoughts about it. The labels *contemplation*, *meditation*, and *exploration* are good synonyms for reflection.

Secondly, although prose devotionals are less likely to be affective or emotional than lyric poems are, this is less true than we might think.

16

Many of the devotionals in this anthology have a strong emotional undertow. The idiom is sometimes exclamatory, but even when it is not, we find ourselves deeply moved by the content. It was the intention of the authors that the wellsprings of emotion would be awakened within us. We rightly think of a devotional reading as giving us a spiritual uplift, which is a way of saying that we are moved by it.

Some devotional genres are not *intended* to be devotionals, but we can *assimilate* them as devotionals by reading them in a certain way. For example, several of the selections in this anthology are prayers. A prayer is addressed to God, not to us, but we can nonetheless read it as a reflection on the godly life. The burial service for the dead in the Anglican Prayer Book is not *designed* to be read as a devotional, but in fact it is a moving meditation of human mortality and immortality. Again, creeds are formulated for the purpose of codifying Christian beliefs, but they can be pondered in a meditative way that transforms them into a devotional exercise.

An event or person can be a form of devotional—a real-life inspiration and prompt to godly living. My explications in this anthology usually provide information about the author of the devotional passage, and often these biographical nuggets become part of the total devotional effect.

The foregoing list of devotional genres is not exhaustive. Additional ones will emerge as this anthology unfolds. The important principle to carry with us is that a text becomes devotional if we approach and absorb it in a certain way.

How Does a Devotional Become a Classic?

This anthology, starting with its title (*The Heart in Pilgrimage: A Treasury of Classic Devotionals on the Christian Life*), elevates the idea of a classic to a position of prominence, so something needs to be said about what a classic is. A written text becomes a classic first of all because of its excellence. A classic in any field is the best within that field. Although this excellence is inherent in the work, and is not conferred upon it by an external committee, a classic is nonetheless acknowledged in culture at large to belong to an elite group. This quality extends to the authors as well as their works. The authors included in this anthology are a roll call of famous writers and people, even though a few are unexpected inclusions in the ranks of devotional writers.

To people familiar with the canon of devotional classics, the titles in the table of contents are likewise famous and therefore classic. These evocative titles are a tempting menu, beckoning us to partake of a feast.

The stylistic features that elevate a devotional piece to the status of a classic fall into the overlapping categories of literary qualities and rhetoric. Verbal beauty and skill with sentence structure come immediately to mind as literary and rhetorical qualities. Even though the passages in this anthology are prose, they often employ poetic techniques such as imagery and metaphor. The imagination is always in quest for originality and freshness of expression, and in fact modern poet T. S. Eliot claimed that poets dislocate language into meaning, doing out-of-routine things with words to overcome the cliché effect of customary ways of expressing truth.[1] A leading ingredient of the explications in this anthology is delineation of the literary and rhetorical techniques by which the authors have achieved their superior impact.

A touchstone by which we can recognize a devotional classic is memorability. We remember the texts printed in this anthology in a way that we do not remember a conventional expository text. It is not a matter of difference in truthfulness but in expression. The memorability of a classic text resides partly in its aphoristic tendency, achieved by such means as a well-turned phrase or a skillfully constructed sentence.

The concluding note in this introduction needs to be a reminder of the function of literature in the human economy. Nineteenth-century American essayist Ralph Waldo Emerson claimed that we all stand in need of expression.[2] We want our affirmations and experiences to be given a voice. Notwithstanding this need for expression, claimed Emerson, adequate expression is rare. Literary authors are sent into the world for the purpose of expression. This points to how we should read the devotionals in this anthology: the authors say what we too want to say, but they say it with greater skill and depth than we can.

1

Finding Rest for Our Restless Heart

AUGUSTINE

You are great, O Lord, and greatly to be praised; great is your power, and infinite your wisdom. Man desires to praise you, for he is a part of your creation. He bears his mortality with him and carries the signs of his sin as proof that you resist the proud. Still, he desires to praise you. . . . You stir him to take delight in praising you, for you have made us for yourself, and our heart is restless until it finds its rest in you. . . . I will seek you, O Lord, and call upon you. I call upon you, O Lord, in my faith which you have given me. . . .

What, therefore, is my God? What, I ask, but the Lord God? . . . Most high, most excellent, most potent, most omnipotent; most merciful and most just; most secret and most truly present; most beautiful and most strong; stable, yet not supported; unchangeable, yet changing all things; never new, never old; making all things new, yet bringing old age upon the proud, and they know it not; always working, ever at rest; gathering, yet needing nothing; sustaining, pervading, and protecting; creating, nourishing, and developing; seeking, and yet possessing all things. . . . You owe men nothing, yet pay out to them as if in debt to your creature, and when you cancel debts, you lose nothing thereby. . . .

Oh! that I might repose in you! Oh! that you would enter into my heart and inebriate it, that I may forget my ills, and embrace you, my sole good! . . . Say unto my soul, I am thy salvation. So speak, that I may hear. . . . Narrow is the mansion of my soul; enlarge it, that you may enter in.

These are the opening words of one of the most famous books in all of history—the *Confessions* of Augustine (354–430). The book as a whole is Augustine's recollection and meditation on the spiritual course of his life. It is the story of a great sinner rescued through a miraculous conversion. The main theme of this quest story is the restless soul, and the passage printed here describes the goal at which Augustine arrived at the end of his quest.

The first thing we notice is that Augustine has embodied his meditation in a prayer addressed directly to God, lending an intimacy to the thoughts that he expresses. The author is not addressing us but God, and in doing so he becomes our representative, saying what we too feel and want to say.

Then we note the intensity of emotion that infuses this devotional passage. Everything is at the white heat of feeling, channeled into an upsurging fountain of praise. The passage uses the same techniques that we find in the praise psalms of the Bible, including ascribing praise to God and listing his praiseworthy attributes and acts. In the second paragraph of the selection, the things ascribed to God keep pouring forth, as though nothing can stop the author's impulse to celebrate the being and works of God. The parallelism of phrases lends artistry and impact to what Augustine says.

Of course the greatest triumph of the passage is the famous aphorism about how *our heart is restless until it finds its rest in* God. It is amazing what all is packed into this sentence. It encapsulates the universal human situation. To be restless without God is not one person's experience but all people's experience. We can confirm the accuracy of Augustine's assertion by taking stock of ourselves.

We should also note the three-part logical sequence that undergirds the statement about the restless heart. In brief, we have (1) a situation described, (2) an explanation for the situation, and (3) a twofold result of these things. The motion of the soul that Augustine describes begins with an action of God, namely, stirring or prompting the human soul to want to praise him. Why does God instill this innate Godward impulse? Because he created people for the purpose of being united to him. So we have a fact stated (the restless soul) along with an explanation underlying the fact (God created us that way). We end this sequence of thinking with a twofold result of the situation that has been declared: (1) the human heart or soul is restless if it rebels against the God-ordained pattern of creaturely praise of the divine, and (2) the human heart finds rest if it accepts the divine order.

The entire passage relies heavily on the rhetorical form of paradox. This is most obvious in the second paragraph, which abounds in seeming contradictions, such as God is *always working* and also *ever at rest*, but there are latent paradoxes in the famous statement about rest and restlessness. The quest of the human soul to find God is also a quest on the part of God to claim the restless soul, inasmuch as he created the situation that Augustine describes. It is also paradoxical that the restlessness that engulfs the unbelieving soul is a blessing, not a curse.[1]

The theme of the restless soul finding rest in God is the subject of one of Jesus's most famous sayings: "Come to me, all who labor and are heavy laden, and I will give you rest. Take my yoke upon you, and learn from me, for I am gentle and lowly in heart, and you will find rest for your souls" (Matt. 11:28–29).

2

How Jesus Is Our Hero

GERARD MANLEY HOPKINS

Our Lord Jesus Christ is our hero, a hero all the world wants. You know how books of tales are written, that put one man before the reader and show him off handsome for the most part and brave and call him My Hero or Our Hero. Often mothers make a hero of a son; girls of a sweetheart and good wives of a husband. Soldiers make a hero of a great general, a party of its leader, a nation of any great man that brings it glory. . . . But Christ . . . is *the* hero.

He too is the hero of a book or books, of the divine Gospels. He is a warrior and a conqueror; of whom it is written he went forth conquering and to conquer. He is a king, Jesus of Nazareth King of the Jews, though when he came to his own kingdom his own did not receive him, and now, his people having cast him off, we Gentiles are his inheritance. . . . He is a thinker, that taught us divine mysteries. He is an orator and poet, as in his eloquent words and parables appears. He is all the world's hero, the desire of nations.

But besides he is the hero of single souls. . . . He is the true-love and the bridegroom of men's souls: the virgins follow him whithersoever he goes; the martyrs follow him through a sea of blood, through great tribulation; all his servants take up their cross and follow him. And those even that do not follow him, yet they look wistfully after him, own him a hero, and wish they dared answer to his call. Children as soon as they can understand ought to be told about him, that they make him the hero of their young hearts. . . .

There met in Jesus Christ all things that can make man lovely and loveable. In his body he was most beautiful. . . . He pleased both God and men daily more and more by his growth of mind and body. But he could not have pleased by growth of body unless the body was the special work of the Holy Ghost. He was not born in nature's course, no man was his father. . . . But his body was framed directly from heaven by the power of the Holy Ghost, of whom it would be unworthy to leave any the least botch or failing in his work. . . . His constitution too was tempered perfectly. . . .

I leave it to you, then, to picture him, in whom the fullness of the godhead dwelt bodily, in his bearing how majestic, how strong and yet how lovely . . . in his limbs, in his look how earnest, grave but kind. In his Passion all this strength was spent, . . . this beauty wrecked, this majesty beaten down. But now it is more than all restored, and for myself I make no secret I look forward with eager desire to seeing the matchless beauty of Christ's body in the heavenly light. . . . He was your maker in time past; hereafter he will be your judge. Make him your hero now. Take some time to think of him; praise him in your hearts.[1]

Gerard Manley Hopkins (1844–1889) is known to the world as a preeminent devotional poet of the Victorian era, but poetry was Hopkins's avocation. His main life's work was as a Jesuit priest and teacher. This devotional on Jesus as our hero is part of a sermon that Hopkins preached on November 23, 1879, at a Catholic church in Bedford Leigh, a suburb of Manchester, England.

The key that unlocks this meditation is to see that it is cast in literary terms, growing out of its author's life as a literary person. Literary scholars know all about the way in which the New Testament Gospels are hero stories, but simply to label them that way is to take the discussion into the study and classroom.

Hopkins shows us in everyday terms how our concept of a hero applies to Jesus. He reminds us of our own experiences of heroes, whether in our reading of stories or in our actual lives. As we read the passage, we assent to everything that Hopkins says about our own creation of heroes and how this fits Jesus perfectly. As Hopkins lists the ways in which Jesus meets the criteria of hero, a portrait of our Lord and Savior cumulatively takes shape. By the time we end Hopkins's exploration of how Jesus fits our concept of a hero, our admiration and love of Jesus are fully awakened. The passage is a masterpiece of hidden persuasion. The appeal at the end to think about Jesus and make him our hero and praise him in our hearts is a perfect action plan and conclusion to the meditation.

⸺◦◦◦⸺

Mark 7:37 strikes the same note about Jesus as Hopkins's meditation does: "And they were astonished beyond measure, saying, 'He has done all things well.'"

3

Exhortation to
Christlike Living

Florence Nightingale

Life is a shallow thing . . . if it lacks depth of religion. . . . If we have not true religious feeling and purpose, life . . . becomes a mere routine and bustle. . . . Our work must be the first thing, but God must be in it. . . . Life is a prayer; and though we pray in our own rooms, in the wards and at church, . . . we have not less but more need of a high standard of duty and of life in our [work]. . . .

Prayer is communion or co-operation with God. . . . But when we speak with God, our power of addressing Him, of holding communion with Him, and listening to His still small voice, depends upon our will being one and the same with His. *Is* He our God, as He was Christ's? To Christ He was all; to us He seems sometimes nothing. Can we retire to rest after our busy, anxious day . . . , with the feeling, "Lord, into Thy hands I commend my spirit?" . . . Can we rise in the morning, almost with a feeling of joy that we are spared another day to do Him service? . . .

Do we think of God as the Eternal, into whose hands we must resign our own souls when we depart hence, and ought to resign our own [souls] as entirely every morning and night of our lives here; with whom live the spirits of the just made perfect, with whom really live . . . our spirits here, and who, in the hour of death, in the hour of life, . . . must be our trust and hope? We would not always be thinking of death, for we must live before we die, and life, perhaps, is as difficult as death. Yet the thought of a time when we shall have passed out of the sight and memory . . . may teach us to rise out of this busy, bustling world, into the clearer light of God's Kingdom. . . .

This is the spirit of prayer, the spirit of conversation or communion with God, which leads us . . . to think of Him, and refer it to Him. When we hear in the voice of conscience *His* voice speaking to us; when we are aware that He is the witness of everything we do, and say, and think, and also the source of every good thing in us . . . ; then God is . . . *with* us. . . .

What is it to live with Christ in God? It is to live in Christ's spirit: forgiving any injuries, real or fancied, from our fellow workers, from those above us as well as from those below . . . ; thirsting after righteousness; . . . doing completely one's duty towards all with whom we have to do . . . ; inclined to be holy as God is holy, perfect as our Father in Heaven is perfect . . . , active, like Christ, in our work; like Christ, meek and lowly in heart . . . ; peacemakers among our companions; . . . placing our spirits in the Father's charge. . . . *This* is to live a life with Christ in God.[1]

Florence Nightingale (1820–1910) is known as the mother of modern nursing. She was a lifelong reader of the Bible, a member of the Church of England, and someone influenced by Methodism. Although born into the privileged class of British society, she felt called by God at the age of seventeen to a life of service. At first she did not know what that service was, but it turned out to be nursing, which at the time was considered a lower class profession. Her stance toward her profession is summed up in a statement she once made to an assembly of nurses: "Christ is the author of our profession."[2]

The example of Florence Nightingale is itself an inspiration and real-life, applied devotional. She turned down a life of privilege and a proposal of marriage in order to serve the suffering. For thirty years she was afflicted by illnesses that largely confined her to her room. Despite this, she continued to make astounding contributions to nursing in England and around the world.

The spiritual side of Florence Nightingale is wonderfully enshrined in a collection of annual addresses composed for "probationers" (nursing students) at the nursing school in London that she founded. These addresses were read to the nurses by the chairman of the Nightingale Fund. Three traits in particular make the addresses inspiring and edifying.

One is the parental stance of Nightingale toward her nursing students, and beyond them to us, her readers. As a spiritual mother, she is both kindly and firm. Regardless of our age, we sense that the author of the words is our spiritual mentor who has earned the right to speak to us with authority.

Second, Nightingale employs a rhetoric of exhortation, which displays two complementary sides. On one side, we are continuously aware of being prodded to be on our guard against complacency in our spiritual lives and vocations in the world.

Third, this note of warning is balanced by encouragement to reach for a high level of attainment in our spiritual lives. There is a tone of buoyant idealism in Nightingale's words. The effect is similar to that of the New Testament epistles, where we are continuously called to our higher selves. Nightingale's goal is totally clear: she wants us to be all that we can be in our spiritual lives, which for her is to be Christlike in our thoughts and actions. Her words are a spiritual pep talk.

Florence Nightingale's life and her exhortation to Christlike living are encapsulated in 1 John 2:6: "Whoever says he abides in [Christ] ought to walk in the same way in which he walked."

4

For Whom the Bell Tolls

John Donne

This bell tolling softly for another says to me, Thou must die. Perchance he for whom this bell tolls may be so ill as that he knows not it tolls for him. And perchance . . . they who are about me, and see my state, may have caused it to toll for me, and I know not that.

The church is catholic, universal; so are all her actions. All that she does belongs to all. When she baptizes a child, that action concerns me, for that child is thereby connected to that head which is my head too, and engrafted into that body whereof I am a member. And when she buries a man, that action concerns me. All mankind is of one author, and is one volume. When one man dies, one chapter is not torn out of the book, but translated into a better language; and every chapter must be so translated. God employs several translators; some pieces are translated by age, some by sickness, some by war, some by justice. But God's hand is in every translation. . . .

As therefore the bell that rings to a sermon calls not upon the preacher only, but upon the congregation to come, so this bell calls us all; but how much more me, who am brought so near the door by this sickness. . . . The bell doth toll for him that thinks it doth; and though it intermit again, yet from that minute that that occasion wrought upon him, he is united to God.

No man is an island, entire of itself. Every man is a piece of the continent, a part of the main. If a clod be washed away by the sea, Europe is the less, as well as if a promontory were, as well as if a manor of thy friend's or of thine own were. Any man's death diminishes me, because I am involved in mankind, and therefore never send to know for whom the bell tolls; it tolls for thee. Neither can we call this a begging of misery, or a borrowing of misery, as though we were not miserable enough of ourselves, but must fetch in more from the next house in taking upon us the misery of our neighbors. . . .

Affliction is a treasure, and scarce any man hath enough of it. No man hath affliction enough that is not matured and ripened by it, and made fit for God by that affliction. If a man carry treasure in bullion or in a wedge of gold, and have none coined into current moneys, his treasure will not defray him as he travels. Tribulation is treasure in the nature of it, but it is not current money in the use of it, except we get nearer and nearer our home, heaven, by it. Another man may be sick too, and sick to death, and this affliction may lie in his bowels, as gold in a mine, and be of no use to him. But this bell that tells me of his affliction, digs out and applies that gold to me: if by this consideration of another's danger, I take mine own into contemplation, and so secure myself, by making my recourse to my God, who is our only security.[1]

———⌘———

John Donne (1572–1631) was in his own day a leading English poet and one of the most famous preachers in English ecclesiastical history. In 1623, Donne contracted a life-threatening illness during an epidemic in London. As he lay recovering, the shape of his collection of twenty-three devotionals (published a year later under the title *Devotions upon Emergent Occasions*) took shape in his mind and imagination. Meditation 17, from which the selection here has been taken, is the most famous entry, partly because some of its aphoristic phrases have passed into the active vocabulary of the English-speaking world.

In Donne's day and continuing to the present day, London was and is a city of church bells. Meditation 17 evokes a picture in our imaginations of bells ringing to announce or anticipate an actual death and to summon members of a parish to a funeral service. The tolling of the bells hovers over the meditation and in itself becomes a summons to contemplate our own mortality.

The theme of Donne's meditation is the uses to which we can put our awareness of death. More specifically, Donne contemplates the profit that comes to him in his illness as he is forced to think about the deaths of his neighbors when he hears church bells calling a congregation to a funeral service. With that as the premise, the meditation covers two main subjects. One is the unity of the body of believers and of the whole human race. The second branches out from that: in the speaker's awareness that he is joined to other people, he contemplates his own mortality as he hears the funeral bells that announce a neighbor's death. The last sentence drives the point home.

The passage showcases the qualities of imagination that characterize Donne's poetry as well as his prose. Chief among these is the gift for metaphor. For example, the whole human race is a book, and individual lives are chapters in that book. When a person dies, a chapter is translated into another language. Suffering is money, but is useless on a journey unless we apply it. And so forth.

Donne's meditation leads us to see that it is the universal human lot to die. The opening lines of the world's most famous poem on the subject of time assert the same truth:

> *For everything there is a season, and a time for every*
> *matter under heaven:*
> *a time to be born, and a time to die. (Eccles. 3:1–2)*

5

Communing with God
through Nature

GEORGE WASHINGTON CARVER

As soon as you begin to read the great and loving God out of all forms of existence He has created, both animate and inanimate, then you will be able to converse with Him, anywhere, everywhere, and at all times. Oh, what a fullness of joy will come to you. . . . God is speaking. . . .

I ask the Great Creator silently daily, and often many times per day, to permit me to speak to Him through the three great Kingdoms of the world, which He has created, viz.—the animal, mineral and vegetable Kingdoms; their relations to each other, to us, our relations to them and the Great God who made all of us. . . . I ask Him daily and often momently to give me wisdom, understanding and bodily strength to do His will, hence I am asking and receiving all the time. . . .

We get closer to God as we get more intimately and understandingly acquainted with the things he has created. . . . More and more as we come closer and closer in touch with nature and its teachings are we able to see the Divine and are therefore fitted to interpret correctly the various languages spoken by all forms of nature about us. . . .

First, . . . nature in its varied forms are the little windows through which God permits me to commune with Him, and to

31

see much of His glory, majesty, and power by simply lifting the curtain and looking in.

Second, I love to think of nature as unlimited broadcasting stations, through which God speaks to us every day, every hour and every moment of our lives, if we will only tune in and remain so.

Third, I am more and more convinced, as I search for truth, that no student of nature can "Behold the lilies of the field," or "Look unto the hills," or study even the microscopic wonders of a stagnant pool of water, and honestly declare himself to be an Infidel. . . .

To those who have as yet not learned the secret of true happiness, which is the joy of coming into the closest relationship with the Maker and Preserver of all things: begin now to study the little things in your own door yard, going from the known to the nearest related unknown, for indeed each new truth brings one nearer to God.[1]

The devotional writings of George Washington Carver (c. 1864–1943) come to us from surviving letters. In one of them, Carver recounts what he calls "my simple conversion" at the age of ten. In his own words, "God just came into my heart one afternoon while I was alone in the loft of our big barn, while I was shelling corn. . . . I knelt down by the barrel of corn and prayed as best I could."

Perhaps based on his childhood conversion, through all the public prominence that Carver achieved, he never lost his spiritual affection for young people. As an adult, after a speaking engagement to YMCA groups that came to be called "Carver's boys," he wrote that he "loved those boys because Christ was there."

The umbrella concept of the selection gleaned from several letters is closeness to God. The variations on that theme are contemplations of different ways in which our experiences of nature can become the channel for communing with God. The effect of sharing the lively actions of Carver's mind and soul is that of turning a prism in the light. By the end, we feel that we can follow Carver's encouragement to make God a moment by moment presence through an increased sensitivity to nature.

Carver's imagination gives us metaphors to ponder and unpack. For example, the varied forms of nature are *windows* out of which we can see God, and radio *stations* to which we can listen to the voice of God. Animals, vegetables, and minerals are *kingdoms*. The forms of nature speak *various languages*.

By way of application, Carver speaks of finding God in nature because he was a scientist, but we can all frame the principle of finding God in terms of our own walk of life. What Carver says about nature, a professor can say about history or art or literature or psychology, and a homemaker about the domestic routine, and a construction worker about the process of building something. The distinctive perspective that Carver offers is his encouragement not only to *see* God in our daily routine but also to *commune and converse* with him there.

Underlying Carver's vision is the conviction that God is present in the external world, that we can therefore know God through nature and culture, and that unbelievers are without excuse for ignoring God. Romans 1:20 is a confirming passage: "For [God's] invisible attributes, namely, his eternal power and divine nature, have been clearly perceived, ever since the creation of the world, in the things that have been made. So they are without excuse."

6

Preface to Galatians

MARTIN LUTHER

This most excellent righteousness—that of faith—which God imputes to us through Christ without works . . . is a righteousness hidden in a mystery that the world does not know. . . . This righteousness is heavenly—we receive it from heaven; we do not have it of ourselves; it is worked in us by grace and apprehended by faith, and by it we rise above all laws and works. . . .

So then, do we do nothing to obtain this righteousness? No, nothing at all. Perfect righteousness is to do nothing, to hear nothing, to know nothing of the law or of works, but to know and believe only that Christ has gone to the Father and is no longer visible; that he sits in heaven at the right hand of his Father, not as a judge, but is made by God our wisdom, righteousness, holiness, and redemption; in short that he is our high priest, entreating for us and reigning over us and in us by grace. . . .

I am indeed a sinner, as far as this present life and righteousness are concerned, as I am a child of Adam; where the law accuses me, death reigns over me and wants to ultimately devour me. But I have another righteousness and live above this life—Christ the Son of God, who knows no sin or death but is righteousness and eternal life. By him, this body of mine that is dead will be raised up again and delivered from the bondage of the law and sin and will be sanctified together with my spirit. . . .

This is easy to describe in words but hard to put into practice, for when we are near death or in other agonies of conscience, these two sorts of righteousness come closer together than we would wish. . . . Let us then be careful to learn to discriminate between these two kinds of righteousness. . . . Give no more to the law than is right, but say, "You want to climb up into the kingdom of my conscience, do you, Law? You want to reign over it and reprove sin and take away the joy I have by faith in Christ and drive me to desperation? Keep within your bounds. . . . By the Gospel I am called to share righteousness and everlasting life. I am called to Christ's kingdom, where my conscience is at rest and there is no law, but rather forgiveness of sins, peace, quietness, joy, health, and everlasting life. Do not trouble me in these matters, for I will not let an intolerable tyrant like you reign in my conscience, which is the temple of Christ, the Son of God. He is the King of righteousness and peace, my sweet Savior and Mediator; he will keep my conscience joyful and quiet in the sound, pure doctrine of the Gospel and in the knowledge of Christian and heavenly righteousness. . . ."[1]

The preface of Martin Luther (1483–1546) to his commentary on Galatians is, metaphorically speaking, a founding document of Protestantism. Although it was a passage in Romans that led to Luther's conversion, his work on Galatians, including the preface, was especially influential in sounding the Reformation keynote that sinners are justified by faith in the merits of Christ alone. Luther was so enthusiastic about the Epistle to the Galatians that he called it "my Epistle. I have betrothed myself to it. It is my Katharina [Luther's wife]."[2]

Before we explore the rhetorical techniques that raise the passage above ordinary theological exposition, we should make sure we understand the theological argument. Luther's subject is justification, not sanctification. His main point is that justification is based on faith in Christ's atoning sacrifice for the sinner, not on works that merit salvation. Luther speaks of two types of righteousness, one Christ's righteousness imputed to a believer, and the other righteous works of the law performed by a person. When Luther uses the word *conscience*, he means assurance of salvation, and a leading concern in the preface is how believers can feel secure about their eternal salvation.

Luther's creative imagination here rises above theological exposition. Underlying the quoted passage (a small excerpt from an expansive preface) is an imagined combat between two opponents. At a conceptual level, it is a battle between truth and error, but Luther imagines the situation more graphically than that with such imagery as *kingdom, reigning*, being *delivered from bondage*, and *an intolerant tyrant* who wants to *reign in my conscience* and *devour me*.

Within this military scenario, familiar battle motifs unfold before us. The opening paragraphs picture a citizen of God's peaceable kingdom, resting in Christ's imputed righteousness. Then a threatening tyrant, a personification of law and works, attempts to *climb up into the kingdom* of the believer's conscience. When this happens, the believer under attack utters a battlefield taunt: *You want to climb up into the kingdom of my conscience, do you, Law . . . ? Keep within your bounds.* The primary narrative motif in this imagined battle is not rescue but protection from an attempted invasion. Most of the passage pictures the believer residing in the archetypal safe place of the imputed righteousness of Christ.

Beyond this narrative element, the spiritual language of the passage is beautiful and rapturous. It is the language of redemption, reading more like lyric poetry than theological prose. The preface is a celebration of the soul set free.

An interesting note in the reception history of this preface is that it led to the conversion of hymn writer Charles Wesley. John Bunyan's soul was likewise settled as he began to read the opening pages of Luther's commentary, and he came to treasure Luther's book as second only to the Bible.[3]

Luther's analysis of law versus grace in his preface is corroborated by Galatians 2:16: "We know that a person is not justified by works of the law but through faith in Jesus Christ, so we also have believed in Christ Jesus, in order to be justified by faith in Christ and not by works of the law, because by works of the law no one will be justified."

7

Waiting on God

ANDREW MURRAY

If salvation indeed comes from God, and is entirely His work, just as our creation was, it follows . . . that our first and highest duty is to wait on Him to do that work as it pleases Him. Waiting becomes then the only way to the experience of a full salvation, the only way, truly, to know God as the God of our salvation. . . .

The deep need for this waiting on God lies equally in the nature of man and the nature of God. God, as Creator, formed man to be a vessel in which He could show forth His power and goodness. Man was not to have in himself a fountain of life, or strength, or happiness. . . . Man's glory and blessedness was not to be independent, or dependent upon himself, but dependent on a God of such infinite riches and love. Man was to have the joy of receiving every moment out of the fullness of God. This was his blessedness as an unfallen creature.

When he fell from God, he was still more absolutely dependent on Him. There was not the slightest hope of his recovery out of his state of death, but in God, His power and mercy. It is God alone who began the work of redemption; it is God alone who continues and carries it on each moment in each individual believer. . . . Waiting on God is just as indispensable, and must be just as continuous and unbroken, as the breathing that maintains our natural life.

It is, then, because Christians do not know in their relation to God of their own absolute poverty and helplessness that they have no sense of the need of absolute and unceasing dependence, or of the unspeakable blessedness of continual waiting on God. But when once a believer begins to see it, . . . waiting on God becomes his brightest hope and joy. As he appreciates how God . . . delights to impart His own nature to His child as fully as He can, how God is not weary of each moment keeping charge of his life and strength, he wonders that he ever thought otherwise of God than as a God to be waited on all the day. God unceasingly giving and working; His child unceasingly waiting and receiving: this is the blessed life. . . .

Waiting on God is itself the highest salvation. It is the ascribing to Him the glory of being All; it is the experiencing that He is All to us. . . .

Our private and public prayers are our chief expression of our relation to God: it is in them chiefly that our waiting upon God must be exercised. If our waiting begins by quieting the activities of nature, and being still before God . . . ; if it yields itself to Him in the assurance that He is working and will work in us; if it maintains the place of humility and stillness and surrender, . . . it will indeed become the strength and the joy of the soul.[1]

Andrew Murray (1828–1917) was born in South Africa, which remained his base of operation for what became an international ministry. An adherent of the Dutch Reformed tradition and a leader in the Keswick movement, Murray published over two hundred books. *Waiting on God* typifies these books and can be considered his signature book. Like many of Murray's books, it is devotional in nature and is packaged as thirty-one chapters, each one built around a Bible verse that speaks of waiting on God.

The ultimate greatness of Murray's devotional book is its subject. Waiting on God is a many-sided Christian virtue that the Bible repeatedly commends. As we turn that prism in the light, we come to see that waiting on God variously entails resignation, submission, dependence, receptivity to what God sends, readiness to act when the time comes, patience, expectancy, hope, and eschatological longing. Murray's book of daily devotionals covers all of these, but the foundation on which they all rest is the core principle of waiting on God. Murray analyzes the essence of this waiting in his opening pages, from which the excerpt printed here is taken. As we follow the author's line of thought, we need to be thinking in terms of what it would mean in our own lives if we practiced the kind of waiting that Murray encourages.

The first key that unlocks the passage is to observe the logic that underlies it. We notice, for example, the repeated rhetorical pattern of "if . . . then." Even when this explicit format does not appear, the underlying drift of the passage is to begin with certain truths about the nature of God, people, and salvation, and then show that waiting on God is the necessary posture of soul that we should exercise.

Additionally, Murray employs the time-honored persuasive strategy of making the topic of discussion appealing to the reader. Throughout the passage, Murray makes waiting on God such an attractive choice that as readers we feel that the author is offering us the deal of a lifetime. *Of course* we would want to do as the author exhorts.

A desirable devotional outcome of Murray's foundational thoughts is to use them as a launching pad for conducting our own exploration of the Bible's teaching about waiting on God, using a word search as our guide.

The rhetoric of exhortation that breathes through Murray's words is encapsulated in Psalm 27:14: "Wait on the LORD . . . , and he shall strengthen thine heart: wait, I say, on the LORD" (KJV).

8

The Foundational Principles of the Christian Life

THE WESTMINSTER AND HEIDELBERG CATECHISMS

Westminster Shorter Catechism

Q. What is the chief end of man?
A. Man's chief end is to glorify God, and to enjoy him forever.

Heidelberg Catechism

Q. What is your only comfort in life and in death?
A. That I am not my own,
but belong—
body and soul,
in life and in death—
to my faithful Savior, Jesus Christ.

He has fully paid for all my sins with his precious blood,
and has set me free from the tyranny of the devil.

He also watches over me in such a way
that not a hair can fall from my head
without the will of my Father in heaven;
in fact, all things must work together for my salvation.

Because I belong to him,
Christ, by his Holy Spirit,
>assures me of eternal life
>and makes me wholeheartedly willing and ready
>from now on to live for him.

Q. What do you need to know in order to live and die happily?
A. Three things:
>first, how great my sins and misery are;
>second, how I am delivered from all my sins and misery;
>third, how I am to be thankful to God for such deliverance.[1]

For purposes of this devotional, the three questions and answers are offered as a triptych—a three-part panel in which the parts form a coherent and symmetrical whole. Viewed in this way, the opening questions of the respective catechisms adhere to what C. S. Lewis calls the basic principle of art, namely, the same in the other.[2] The element of sameness that unifies the three items is that they all deal with foundational issues or "first things" in Christian faith and practice. Thus the Shorter Catechism speaks of *chief end* and the Heidelberg Catechism of our *only comfort* (meaning supreme or greatest comfort) and a decisive *three things* that we need to know in order to live and die happily. These formulas let us know that truth has been reduced to its essential core. We feel that we have been handed a survival guide for living.

But within this unity, the three items also differ from each other. Our eye immediately catches the succinctness of the first question and answer, the unexpected expansiveness of the second one, and the intermediate length of the third. A sense of repose accompanies this pleasing arrangement—a feeling that everything is as it should be. There is similar variety and balance at the level of subject matter. The first item focuses on God and human enjoyment of him, while the two questions

41

from the Heidelberg Catechism put the emphasis on people and their need for comfort. An outward gaze is balanced by an introspective one.

We should also take time to admire the verbal beauty that is present. Why have these words reverberated through the centuries? Because they are extraordinary rather than ordinary, beautiful rather than prosaic. They have an aphoristic flair. *Chief end* attracts our attention and sticks in the memory; the modernizing counterpart *primary purpose* is eminently forgettable and diminishes the multiple levels of meaning in the word *end* (that for which someone is created, but also the goal toward which one aspires and final destination at which one arrives).

One of the things that characterizes the classic devotionals found in this anthology is that they possess an "above and beyond" ingredient that raises them above a readily forgotten statement. Often this "value added" ingredient is a surprising or paradoxical element akin to a riddle. We are teased into figuring it out and in the process discover deeper meanings. The three items in this triptych provide illustrations of this principle.

For example, we expect the answer to the question of people's chief end to be glorifying God, but then we are surprised and led to ponder why the authors of the catechism made the enjoyment of God equally important. Furthermore, what is the connection between glorifying God and enjoying him? To phrase our great comfort in terms of not owning ourselves is certainly an original twist, and we further wonder why the answer does not stop with salvation but keeps going full steam ahead on the subjects of providence and willingness to serve Christ. If we were asked what we need to know to live and die well, we would readily reply in terms of the forgiveness of our sins, but the Heidelberg Catechism instead gives three answers covering the whole of Christian living. In these ways and additional ones, we are impressed by how much better the catechisms express the issues than most people would.

For those who grew up with these catechisms, the words are hallowed, both in themselves and by association. The three questions and answers have such inner power that they can become similarly revered by anyone who lives with them and ponders them.

The underlying theme of the three questions and answers is the importance of foundational principles in the Christian life. Moses's words to his nation as recorded in Deuteronomy 11:18–20 are a famous passage on this theme: "You shall therefore lay up these words of mine in your heart and in your soul. . . . You shall teach them to your children . . . [and] write them on the doorposts of your house and on your gates."

9

The Imitation of Christ

Thomas à Kempis

When Jesus is present, all is well, and nothing seems hard, but when Jesus is not present, everything is hard. When Jesus does not speak to our heart, all comfort is worthless, but if Jesus speaks but a single word, great is our comfort. Did not Mary Magdalene rise up quickly from the place where she wept when Martha said to her, The Master has come and calls for you? Happy hour when Jesus calls you from tears to the joy of the spirit! How dry and hard you are without Jesus! How senseless and empty if you desire anything beyond Jesus! Is not this greater loss than if you should lose the whole world?

What can the world offer you without Jesus? To be without Jesus is hell most grievous, and to be with Jesus is a sweet paradise. If Jesus is with you, no enemy can harm you. Whoever finds Jesus finds a great treasure, yea, a good above all good; and he who loses Jesus loses much, yea, more than the whole world. Poorest of all is the one who lives without Jesus, and richest of all is the one who is close to Jesus.

It is great art to know how to live with Jesus, and to know how to hold Jesus is great wisdom. Be humble and peaceable, and Jesus will be with you. Be godly and quiet, and Jesus will remain with you. You will quickly drive Jesus away and lose His favor if you turn away to worldly things. And if you have put Him to flight and lost Him, to whom will you flee, and whom wilt thou seek for a friend? . . . If Jesus is not your friend above all, you will be sad and desolate. It is therefore folly to trust . . . in any other. It is better to have the whole world against you, than that Jesus be offended with you. Therefore, of all who are dear to you, let Jesus be loved above all.

Let all be loved for Jesus' sake, but Jesus for His own. Jesus Christ alone is to be supremely loved, for He alone is found good and faithful above all friends. For His sake and in Him let both enemies and friends be dear to you, and pray for them all that they may all know and love Him. . . .

You ought to bring a pure and clean heart to God, if you desire to be ready to see how gracious the Lord is. . . . When the grace of God comes to a person, then he becomes able to do all things, but when it departs, he will be poor and weak and given up unto troubles. When this happens, do not be cast down, nor despair, but rest with calm mind on the will of God, and bear all things that come upon you to the praise of Jesus Christ; for after winter comes summer, after night day returns, and after the tempest comes a great calm.[1]

The Imitation of Christ is one of the most famous devotional books of all time. Multiple sources claim that it is the second best seller behind the Bible and also the most widely translated book next to the Bible. The author, Thomas à Kempis (1380–1471), was a Catholic monk of Dutch-German extraction. *The Imitation of Christ* is an encyclopedic book comprised of a hundred individual meditations covering the whole of the spiritual life.

The unifying theme of the excerpt printed here is that embracing Jesus is the one thing necessary in life. The author outlines a great either-or, a spiritual fork in the road, that confronts every person. Choosing to follow Jesus leads to life, and refusing to follow him leads to ruin. The rhetorical or persuasive strategy that permeates the passage flows from this contrast. On one side, the author makes the benefits of following Christ so appealing that we can speak of the rhetoric of enticement. On the other side is the rhetoric of warning, as Thomas sounds an alarm about the dire results of choosing something other than Christ.

This carefully constructed contrast fits the devotional purpose of strengthening our love for Christ and our devotion to him. The believing soul is left with a feeling of gratitude for the treasure that is possessed in Christ. This passage does not speak directly about the topic named in the book's title, namely, the imitation of Christ. Instead, the passage delineates the prerequisite for imitating Christ: we will want to imitate Christ only if we have made him the Lord of our lives.

The New Testament makes it clear that the very essence of the Christian life is to follow Christ and imitate him in all our actions. This principle is encapsulated in the apostle Paul's command to the Corinthians: "Be imitators of me, as I am of Christ" (1 Cor. 11:1).

10

Two Prayers

SAMUEL JOHNSON

Easter, April 16, 1775

Almighty God, heavenly Father, whose mercy is over all Thy works, look with pity on my miseries and sins.

Suffer me to commemorate, in thy presence, my redemption by Thy Son Jesus Christ.

Enable me so to repent of my misspent time, that I may pass the residue of my life in Thy fear, and to Thy glory.

Relieve, O Lord, as seems best unto Thee, the infirmities of my body, and the perturbation of my mind.

Fill my thoughts with awful love of Thy goodness, with just fear of Thine anger, and with humble confidence in Thy mercy.

Let me study Thy laws, and labor in the duties which Thou shalt set before me.

Take not from me Thy Holy Spirit, but incite in me such good desires as may produce diligent endeavors after Thy glory and my own salvation.

And when, after hopes and fears, and joys and sorrows, thou shalt call me hence, receive me to eternal happiness for the sake of Jesus Christ our Lord. Amen.

Sunday, December 5, 1784
[one week before Johnson's death]

Almighty and most merciful Father, I am now as to human eyes it seems, about to commemorate, for the last time, the death of thy Son Jesus Christ our Savior and Redeemer.

Grant, O Lord, that my whole hope and confidence may be in his merits, and thy mercy; enforce and accept my imperfect repentance; make this commemoration available to the confirmation of my faith, the establishment of my hope, and the enlargement of my charity; make the death of thy Son Jesus Christ effectual to my redemption.

Have mercy upon me, and pardon the multitude of my offences.

Bless my friends; have mercy upon all men.

Support me, by thy Holy Spirit, in the days of my weakness and at the hour of death.

Receive me, at my death, to everlasting happiness, for the sake of Jesus Christ. Amen.[1]

Samuel Johnson (1709–1784) is a towering figure of English literature, being a poet, literary critic, writer of prose fiction, and compiler of a dictionary. Johnson's *Prayers and Meditations* (from which the entries here were taken) was published a year after his death. The prayers and meditations were composed over some fifty years on occasions such as Easter and the author's birthday. The second prayer printed here was composed a week before Johnson's death, with Johnson signaling his awareness that he was about to commemorate holy communion for the last time.

A published prayer can become a devotional reading in three ways. First, we can read the words as a prayer, allowing the author to be our representative, saying what we ourselves want to say to God, only saying it better than we can. Second, the words can become a meditation on the spiritual life, as we ponder the statements individually and allow them to stimulate us to thought. Third, to borrow a formula from John

Milton, we can allow the words and sentiments to set our thoughts and feelings "in right tune."[2]

The style of a devotional reading is part of its effect, and that is where Johnson's prayers shine. Johnson's style exudes verbal beauty. It is a formal style, matching the gravity of the religious content. The most obvious manifestations of the formal style are the elevated words, long sentences, parallel phrases and clauses within a sentence, balance of sentence elements, and a rhythmic, wavelike rise and fall of language. All of these elements produce an aphoristic, memorable quality, heightened by being printed as a succession of sentences instead of a single paragraph.

At the level of content, Johnson's prayers prompt us to reflect on questions such as the following: What are the most important petitions we should ask of God? What would our own petitions be if we knew that we would die within a week? How can we pray with a reverence appropriate for speaking to God?

The format of Johnson's prayers is a catalog or list of petitions. Many Old Testament psalms employ the same technique, lending a familiar quality to Johnson's prayers. Psalm 51 may have been a model for Johnson:

> *Have mercy on me, O God,*
>   *according to your steadfast love; . . .*
> *Cast me not away from your presence,*
>   *and take not your Holy Spirit from me.*
> *Restore to me the joy of your salvation,*
>   *and uphold me with a willing spirit. (Ps. 51:1, 11–12)*

11

Jesus Our Guide
and Guardian

John Henry Newman

The meditation. There are some who think that God is so great that He disdains to look down upon us, our doings and our fortunes. But He who did not find it beneath His Majesty to make us, does not think it beneath Him to observe and to visit us. He says Himself in the Gospel: "Are not five sparrows sold for two farthings? And not one of them is forgotten before God. Yea, the very hairs of your head are all numbered. Fear not, therefore: you are of more value than many sparrows." He determined from all eternity that He would create us. He settled our whole fortune. . . .

He died for us all upon the Cross that . . . we might be saved. And He calls upon us lovingly, begging us to accept the benefit of His meritorious and most Precious Blood. And those who trust Him He takes under His special protection. He marks out their whole life for them; He appoints all that happens to them. He guides them in such a way as to secure their salvation; He gives them just so much of health, of wealth, of friends, as is best for them; He afflicts them only when it is for their good; He is never angry with them. He measures out just that number of years which is good for them; and He appoints the hour of their death in such a way as to secure their perseverance up to it.

The prayer. O my Lord and Savior, in Thy arms I am safe; keep me and I have nothing to fear; give me up and I have nothing to hope for. I know not what will come upon me before I die. I know nothing about the future, but I rely upon Thee. I pray Thee to give me what is good for me; I pray Thee to take from me whatever may imperil my salvation. . . . O Thou who didst die on the Cross for me, even for me, sinner as I am, give me to know Thee, to believe on Thee, to love Thee, to serve Thee; ever to aim at setting forth Thy glory; to live to and for Thee; to set a good example to all around me; give me to die just at that time and in that way which is most for Thy glory, and best for my salvation.[1]

⎯⎯⎯⎯⎯⎯

John Henry Newman (1801–1890) was a prominent Catholic of the Victorian era. He had a varied career as priest, theologian, and educator. Newman was a prolific author on many subjects. The devotional reading printed here (titled "Jesus Our Guide and Guardian" by Newman himself) is from a book compiled and published three years after his death, titled *Meditations and Devotions.*

The format of Newman's meditation has a winsome simplicity and orderliness. The first paragraph lays a doctrinal foundation by asserting that God cares for us in every detail of our lives. The second paragraph makes the doctrine concrete to our imaginations by listing God's acts of providence, including ones that we do not ordinarily consider. The meditation flows seamlessly into the majestic culminating prayer. It is structured as a catalog or list of petitions addressed to Christ. Even on a first reading we are aware of how subtly the petitions echo and match the acts of providence that were covered in the meditation that has preceded.

Newman's style has been praised for its combined elegance and simplicity. The overall effect is one of majesty. The sentences, for example, are long and stately. The format consists of parallel clauses strung in linear fashion, highlighted by patterns of repetition. In the second paragraph, for example, we find the sequence *He marks, He takes, He guides, He gives.* Similarly, in the prayer we find the parallel

constructions *give me to know Thee, . . . to love Thee, to serve Thee.*
Even though the content of meditation and prayer is simple and humble, the cumulative effect of the catalog format and the parallelism and
repetition of phraseology gradually becomes a quiet crescendo. The
passage is modest in length, but so many individual items are included
that we end with a feeling of abundance.

---

*Newman's meditation and prayer instill in us a confidence that
Jesus is sufficient to supply our needs, especially in regard to
our spiritual destiny. Second Peter 1:3 is a celebration of this
same confidence: "His divine power has granted to us all things
that pertain to life and godliness, through the knowledge of him
who called us to his own glory and excellence."*

12

Bidding Prayer

Beloved in Christ,

This Christmas Eve it is our duty and delight
to prepare ourselves to hear again the message of the angels,
and to go in heart and mind to Bethlehem,
and see this thing which is come to pass,
and the Babe lying in a manger.

Therefore let us hear again from Holy Scripture
the tale of the loving purposes of God from the first days of
our sin
until the glorious redemption brought us by this holy Child;
and let us make this house of prayer glad with our carols of
praise.

But first, because this of all things would rejoice Jesus' heart,
let us pray to him for the needs of the whole world, and all his
people;
for peace upon the earth he came to save;
for love and unity within the one Church he did build;
for goodwill among all peoples.

And particularly at this time let us remember
the poor, the cold, the hungry, the oppressed;

the sick and them that mourn; the lonely and the unloved;
the aged and the little children;
and all who know not the Lord Jesus, or who love him not,
or who by sin have grieved his heart of love.

Lastly let us remember all those who rejoice with us,
but upon another shore and in a greater light,
that multitude which no one can number,
whose hope was in the Word made flesh,
and with whom, in this Lord Jesus, we for evermore are one.

These prayers and praises let us humbly offer up to the throne
of heaven,
in the words that Christ himself has taught us.

Our Father, which art in heaven,
    hallowed be thy name,
    thy kingdom come, thy will be done,
    on earth as it is in heaven.
Give us this day our daily bread.
And forgive us our trespasses,
    as we forgive them that trespass against us.
And lead us not into temptation,
    but deliver us from evil.

Amen.

The Almighty God bless us with his grace;
Christ give us the joys of everlasting life;
and unto the fellowship of the citizens above
may the King of Angels bring us all.[1]

The quaint term *bidding prayer* refers to a specific format for prayer in a public setting. A minister "bids" or instructs a congregation to pray for the items that he lists individually. Either the assembled people pray silently after each item is named, or the leader expresses the petitions on behalf of the congregation. In both cases, a bidding prayer uses the rhetorical formula of the command *Let us*. . . .

A Christmas Eve service known as Lessons and Carols had its origin in 1918 at King's College Chapel, part of Cambridge University in England. Since then, the festival has been held annually around the world right to the present day, with the same basic content and format. The customary processional hymn is "Once in Royal David's City." After the procession is finished, with everyone standing, the presiding minister leads the congregation in the bidding prayer. The whole occasion makes the prayer an electrifying experience, but even without that celebrative atmosphere, the prayer makes a moving private devotional.

We immediately note the stately beauty of the words and lines. Like the language of the King James Bible (which doubtless influenced the composer of the prayer), the language of the bidding prayer is elegant without being stilted. We can say further that it combines simplicity with majesty.

To worshipers who are familiar with this bidding prayer, hearing it every year at a Christmas service is like renewing acquaintance with an esteemed friend. But if we look carefully at how the prayer unfolds, we can see that it is a carefully contrived structure of surprises and retarding devices. The whole purpose of the lessons and carols service is to get to the lessons and carols, but this prayer holds us back, creating a sense of suspense. Paradoxically, because these units are detours from our eventual destination of lessons and carols, our attention is riveted on each holding pattern.

For example, the second stanza invites us to listen to the nativity story from the Gospels, but then the third stanza begins, *but first* let us pray for the needs of the world. Then, just as we have completed praying for the needs of the world, another category of people is introduced (the most needy members of society). With that task completed, we soar in our imaginations as we remember departed saints in heaven. Then we are invited to pray the Lord's Prayer. Surely that completes the list, we say to ourselves. But no, there is one more closing prayer. As we traverse this varied territory, the range of coverage is breathtaking.

Three avenues exist by which to assimilate this prayer as a devotional. First, we can experience the language as an experience of the beauty of holiness. Second, a prayer is always an appropriate vehicle for a devotional meditation and uplift. Finally, only the first stanza is directly related to Christmas; after that, the topics are universal and always worthy of our contemplation and prayer.

———✸✸✸———

Bidding prayers are intercessory in nature, meaning that they are prayers uttered on behalf of others. First Timothy 2:1, 3–4 is a biblical command to engage in such intercession: "I urge that supplications, prayers, intercessions, and thanksgivings be made for all people. . . . This is good, and it is pleasing in the sight of God our Savior, who desires all people to be saved and to come to the knowledge of the truth."

13

True and Substantial Wisdom

John Calvin

True and substantial wisdom principally consists of two parts, the knowledge of God, and the knowledge of ourselves. . . . No man can take a survey of himself but he must immediately turn to the contemplation of God, in whom he "lives and moves;" since it is evident that the talents which we possess are not from ourselves, and that our very existence is nothing but a subsistence in God alone. These bounties, distilling to us by drops from heaven, form, as it were, so many streams conducting us to the fountain-head. Our poverty conduces to a clearer display of the infinite fullness of God. The knowledge of ourselves, therefore, is not only an incitement to seek after God, but likewise a considerable assistance towards finding him. . . .

By the knowledge of God, I intend not merely a notion that there is such a being, but also an acquaintance with whatever we ought to know concerning Him, conducing to his glory and our benefit. . . . It is one thing to understand that God our Maker supports us by his power, governs us by his providence, nourishes us by his goodness, and follows us with blessings of every kind, and another to embrace the grace of reconciliation proposed to us in Christ. . . .

Though our mind cannot conceive of God without ascribing some worship to him, it will not be sufficient merely to apprehend that he is the only proper object of universal worship and adoration, unless we are also persuaded that he is the fountain of all good, and seek for none but in him. This I maintain, not only because he sustains the universe . . . by his infinite power, governs it by his wisdom, preserves it by his goodness, and especially reigns over the human race in righteousness and judgment . . . ; but because there cannot be found the least particle of wisdom, light, righteousness, power, rectitude, or sincere truth which does not proceed from him, and claim him for its author.

We should therefore learn to expect and supplicate all these things from him, and thankfully to acknowledge what he gives us. For this sense of the divine perfections is calculated to teach us piety. . . . By piety, I mean a reverence and love of God, arising from a knowledge of his benefits.[1]

⸺⸺

The first thing we need to know about this passage is the importance of the book in which it appears. *The Institutes of the Christian Religion,* written by John Calvin (1509–1564), is one of the most influential books in the history of Christianity. Along with Martin Luther, John Calvin was the foremost Protestant Reformer. Calvin's *Institutes* is a book of instruction in the basics of Reformation theology. As seen from the excerpt taken from the opening paragraphs, Calvin invites us to join him in thinking through the issues about which he writes.

The famous opening sentence of Calvin's landmark book ranks as one of the famous aphorisms of Christian writing, along the lines of Augustine's statement about how our souls are restless till they rest in God. Someone has aptly said that Calvin's sentence about true and substantial wisdom "alone is worth a lifetime's contemplation."[2] Still more weightiness attaches to Calvin's opening sentence when we learn that it takes its place in a distinguished tradition of earlier formulations of the key idea that knowledge of God and ourselves is what we most need to navigate life.

Before leaving the opening sentence, we can profitably ponder it. Why does Calvin single out these two topics as constituting true wisdom? Why does he put knowledge of God and ourselves on a par instead of choosing knowledge of God as supreme? As we share Calvin's meditation on ultimate matters, we have our own understanding pushed in unexpected directions.

Once stated, the opening idea of dual knowledge unifies the entire passage. While the passage speaks more about God than us, a portrait of our creaturely nature and standing toward God also emerges. God is portrayed as all-sufficient and beneficent, and people as needy and insufficient.

The topics unfold according to the following pattern by paragraphs: (1) when we look at ourselves, we see our need for God and are prompted to seek him; (2) our knowledge of God cannot be mere head knowledge but must be experiential and must embrace God's gracious offer of salvation; (3) God is worthy of our total commitment because he is the source of all our good; (4) by way of application, we must live in a stance of dependence and gratitude toward this beneficent God. Thinking about these ideas adds up to an edifying devotional exercise.

Calvin writes here in a high style that elevates the God about whom he writes. We find long sentences comprised of lists of grand attributes and acts, phrased as parallel sentence parts. Repeatedly as the passage unfolds, we are swept onward by the mighty stream on which we have embarked. While being cast as a statement about the knowledge most worth having, the passage is also doxological, praising God as the source of all good.

The contrast that this devotional passage draws between people and God is not between sinfulness and perfection, but rather between creaturely dependence and divine satisfaction of what people need. 2 Corinthians 3:5 expresses this same twofold truth: "Not that we are sufficient in ourselves to claim anything as coming from us, but our sufficiency is from God."

14

What Christians Believe

THE APOSTLES' CREED

I believe in God the Father almighty,
maker of heaven and earth;

And in Jesus Christ his only Son our Lord, who was
    conceived by the Holy Ghost,
    born of the Virgin Mary,
    suffered under Pontius Pilate,
    was crucified, dead and buried;
    he descended into hell;
    the third day he rose again from the dead;
    he ascended into heaven,
    and sits on the right hand of God the Father almighty;
    from thence he shall come to judge the living and the dead.
I believe in
    the Holy Spirit;
    the holy catholic church;
    the communion of saints;
    the forgiveness of sins;
    the resurrection of the body,
    and the life everlasting.

Everyone knows that the Apostles' Creed is a summary of Christian doctrine and an ecumenical statement of faith, but is it also a devotional reading? That is a good question, and it has a good answer. Like the Lord's Prayer, the Apostles' Creed lends itself to assimilating at a slow and contemplative pace. Each item in the Creed deserves to be dwelt upon and unpacked. Because we already know the Creed by heart, we can close our eyes and think and be moved as we work our way through the successive statements.

The origins of this famous document are shrouded in mystery. A forerunner existed in the early Latin era of the Christian church. The earliest known mention of the expression "Apostles' Creed" occurs in a letter of 390 from the Synod of Milan.

Is the Apostles' Creed prose or verse? It is prose, but when we read it, and even more when we recite it orally, it is experienced as poetry. Why is this so? Because of the abundance of short parallel clauses and phrases that create the effect of composition by lines the way poetry is composed. Even when it is not printed as it is here, we experience the Apostles' Creed as structured on the poetic principle of short lines.

One feature of artistic or literary prose (as distinct from everyday expository prose) is that it invites multiplicity of interpretation. Often this starts with the structure of a passage. Some religious groups divide the Apostles' Creed into twelve statements. If we take a wide-angle view, the Creed falls naturally into a Trinitarian framework. Working the other way, a detailed breakdown of the Creed yields seventeen or eighteen articles.

I've chosen this printed format of the Creed for rhetorical considerations. There are two *I believe in* main clauses. We find five statements about Jesus that complete the verb *was*. That series is followed by four parallel sentences that name what Jesus did following his resurrection, and in an additional nuance, we can see that these four actions cover past, present, and future. Furthermore, we experience a descent as we contemplate the events surrounding the passion of Jesus, and then an ascent beginning with *the third day he rose again from the dead*. Finally, the second appearance of *I believe in* is followed by a buoyant list of six succinct parallel phrases naming items of belief.

We should not downplay the importance of the rhetorical and artistic beauty of the Apostles' Creed. Perfection of form always adds to the effect of an utterance. The Apostles' Creed would not hold the place that it has always held in Christendom without the beauty that has crowned it as a benediction. A summary of its stylistic excellence is the oft-quoted statement that the Apostles' Creed expresses Christian truth "in sublime simplicity, in unsurpassable brevity, in beautiful order, and with liturgical solemnity."[1]

———∞∞∞———

The tradition that each of the twelve apostles contributed an article to the Apostles' Creed is totally fanciful, but the Creed is demonstrably a succinct summary of what the apostles taught and what Christians have always believed. In the events surrounding Pentecost, we read that the converts "devoted themselves to the apostles' teaching and the fellowship" (Acts 2:42).

15

Following the Steps
of the Master

HARRIET BEECHER STOWE

In many private histories, there are Gethsemanes. There are visitations of sudden, overpowering, ghastly troubles; troubles that transcend all ordinary human sympathy, such as the helpless human soul has to wrestle with alone. And it was because . . . such crushing experiences are to be meted out to the children of men that infinite love provided us with a divine Friend who had been through the deepest of them all, and come out victorious.

In the sudden wrenches which come by the entrance of death into our family circles, there is often an inexplicable depth of misery that words cannot tell. No outer words tell what a trial is to the soul. Only Jesus, who, as the Head of the human race, united in himself every capability of human suffering, and proved them all, in order that he might help us, only He has an arm strong enough, and a voice tender enough to reach us.

The stupor of the disciples in the agony of Jesus [in Gethsemane] is a sort of parable or symbol of the inevitable loneliness of the deepest kind of sorrow. There are friends, loving, honest, true, but they cannot watch with us through such hours. It is like the hour of death—nobody can go with us.

But he who knows what it is so to suffer; he who has felt the horror, the amazement, the heart-sick dread; who has fallen on his face overcome, and prayed with cryings and tears, and the bloody sweat of agony, He can understand us, and can help us. He can send an angel from heaven to comfort us when every human comforter is "sleeping for sorrow." The Father gave Jesus the power to bring many sons and daughters unto glory.

And it may comfort us under such trials to hope that as he thus gained an experience and a tenderness which made him mighty to comfort and to save, so we, in our humbler measure, may become comforters to others. We may find ourselves with hearts tenderer to feel, and stronger to sustain others; even as the apostle says, he "comforteth us in all our tribulations, that we may be able to comfort them that are in any trouble, by the comfort wherewith we ourselves are comforted of God" (2 Cor. 1:4).[1]

Harriet Beecher Stowe (1811–1896) was a famous abolitionist and prolific American author. She wrote a dozen novels and more than twice as many nonfiction books. Her novel *Uncle Tom's Cabin* is not only Stowe's signature book but also one of the most famous books in the world. When President Abraham Lincoln met Stowe, he is reported to have said, "So you're the little woman who wrote the book that made this great war."[2]

The excerpt printed here comes from Stowe's remarkable book *Footsteps of the Master*. It is not a conventional "life of Christ" but a book that traces the presence of Christ in the Bible from Old Testament appearances and prophecies through his return at the end of history. The book is informed by thorough research into the topic, but this triumph of scholarship is concealed by the simple, straightforward style and absence of scholarly notes.

The devotional aspect of *Footsteps of the Master* is always present alongside the factual data from the Bible, and in this respect the entry printed here epitomizes the book. Stowe's approach is to present Jesus as an example in whose steps we can and must follow. The selection comes from the section devoted to Christ's suffering in Gethsemane, and in a deft example of bridge-building, Stowe speaks of the metaphoric *Gethsemanes* of everyone's life.

The subject of the passage is the nature of suffering and how to endure it. The empathy with which Stowe describes the universal suffering that is the human lot belongs to what classical rhetoric called *pathos*—an appeal to a reader's imagination and feelings. Having made us feel the personal and universal experience of solitary suffering, Stowe offers a pathway to victory by reminding us of the example of Jesus in Gethsemane. The passage strikes a balance between a realistic acknowledgment of how terrible our sufferings sometimes are and encouragement to hope that we can suffer as Jesus did and triumph as he did.

First Peter 2:21 encapsulates the same truth as Stowe's meditation on the meaning of Gethsemane in our personal life: "Christ also suffered for you, leaving you an example, so that you might follow in his steps."

16

A Serious Call to a Devout and Holy Life

WILLIAM LAW

Devotion signifies a life given, or devoted, to God. The devout person is one who lives no longer to his own will, or the way and spirit of the world, but to the sole will of God, who considers God in everything, who serves God in everything, who makes all the parts of his common life parts of piety, by doing everything in the Name of God. . . .

As sure as it is our duty to look wholly unto God in our prayers, so sure is it that it is our duty to live wholly unto God in our lives. We can no more be said to live unto God, unless we live unto Him in all the ordinary actions of our life . . . than we can be said to pray unto God, unless our prayers look wholly unto Him. . . . As a good Christian should consider every place as holy, because God is there, so he should look upon every part of his life as a matter of holiness, because it is to be offered unto God. . . . Worldly business is to be made holy unto the Lord, by being done as a service to Him, and in conformity to His Divine will.

For as all men, and all things in the world, as truly belong unto God as any places, things, or persons that are devoted to divine service [in the church], so all things are to be used, and all persons are to act in their several states and employments, for the glory of God. . . .

It is for lack of considering this that we see such a mixture of ridicule in the lives of many people. You see them strict as to some times and places of devotion, but when the service of the Church is over, they are like those that seldom or never come there. In their way of life, their manner of spending their time and money, in their cares and fears, in their pleasures and indulgences, in their labor and diversions, they are like the rest of the world. . . . Their devotion goes no farther than their prayers, and when they are over, they live no more unto God, till the time of prayer returns again.

Men and women, rich and poor, must, with bishops and priests, walk before God in the same wise and holy spirit, . . . and in the same discipline and care of their souls; not only because they have all the same rational nature, and are servants of the same God, but because they all want the same holiness, to make them fit for the same happiness, to which they are all called. It is therefore absolutely necessary for all Christians, whether men or women, to consider themselves as persons that are devoted to holiness, and so order their common ways of life, by such rules of reason and piety as may turn it into continual service unto Almighty God.[1]

"What's in a name?" asks Shakespeare's fictional character Juliet.[2] What's in a title? we might equally well ask. The answer in both cases is "a great deal." Surely we experience the list of titles in this anthology as a tempting menu of intriguing topics. The titles themselves can yield a devotional experience, and in many cases we are led to wonder how the author will develop the idea named in the title.

The title that William Law (1686–1761) chose for his famous book first compels our attention by claiming to be not just a call to a holy life but a *serious* call. "What does that signal?" we wonder. Furthermore, because in the annals of famous devotional writings there is an undertow of otherworldly spirituality and withdrawal from the active life, we wonder if Law's call to holiness will tend in that direction. As is true of most of the selections in this anthology, Law's call to a holy life springs a surprise on us.

William Law began his professional life as a Church of England cleric. The dictates of his conscience cost him his church position, with the result that from the age of twenty-eight he lived a varied life, serving as a tutor, overseeing charitable works, and writing voluminously. His *Serious Call to a Devout and Holy Life* elicited the admiration of such contemporaries as John Wesley, Samuel Johnson, and William Wilberforce.

Law's goal is to awaken Christians from their spiritual lethargy. Looking for this element of critique is a good preliminary piece of analysis we can perform on the excerpted passage. This spirit of critique is where the word *serious* enters the picture: Law wants the common person (his intended audience) to get serious about the Christian life. And what would that look like? It means refusing to limit spirituality to specifically religious actions like prayer and devotions and instead bringing our best energies to living for God in *all* of life. Consistency between our devotional life and our practical life is Law's serious call, and it results in an elevation of the common person and common life to ultimate spiritual significance.

The prevailing view that Law's style is simple and direct is misleading. His sentences are long and filled with parallel clauses. A rigorous logic of equation underlies the excerpted passage, as repeatedly we are asked to see that what applies to the life of prayer and worship applies equally to our daily life in the world. The principle of "as . . . so" recurs.

William Law's book belongs to the genre known as a formal call to holiness. This familiar biblical genre is well illustrated by 1 Peter 1:15–16: "As he who called you is holy, you also be holy in all your conduct, since it is written, 'You shall be holy, for I am holy.'"

17

Practicing the Presence of God

Brother Lawrence

There is not in the world a kind of life more sweet and delightful than that of a continual conversation with God. . . . If we only knew the need we have of the grace and assistance of God, we should never lose sight of Him, no, not for a moment. . . . I cannot imagine how religious persons can live satisfied without the practice of the presence of God. . . .

I do not say that we must put any violent constraint upon ourselves. No, we must serve God in a holy freedom; we must do our business faithfully, without trouble or disquiet, recalling our mind to God mildly and with tranquility, as often as we find it wandering from Him. . . . Even some particular forms of devotion, though very good in themselves, [can be engaged in] unreasonably. [Formal] devotions are only means to attain to the end; so when by this exercise of the presence of God we are with Him who is our end, it is then useless to return to the means. . . . At the first, one often thinks it lost time [to practice the presence of God]; but you must go on, and resolve to persevere in it to death, notwithstanding all the difficulties that may occur. . . .

God requires no great matters of us; a little remembrance of Him from time to time, a little adoration: sometimes to pray for His grace, sometimes to offer Him your sufferings, and sometimes to return Him thanks for the favors He has given you, and still gives you, in the midst of your troubles, and to console yourself with Him the oftenest you can. Lift up your heart to Him, sometimes even at your meals, and when you are in company; the least little remembrance will always be acceptable to Him. You need not cry aloud; He is nearer to us than we are aware.

It is not necessary for being with God to be always at church; we may make an oratory of our heart, wherein to retire from time to time, to converse with Him in meekness, humility, and love. Everyone is capable of such familiar conversation with God, some more, some less. He knows what we can do. Let us begin then; perhaps He expects but one generous resolution on our part. Have courage. . . .

Use yourself then by degrees thus to worship Him, to beg His grace, to offer Him your heart from time to time, in the midst of your business, even every moment if you can. Do not always scrupulously confine yourself to certain rules, or particular forms of devotion, but act with a general confidence in God, with love and humility.[1]

When we see the titles of the classic devotional works that appear in this anthology, we mistakenly picture all of them as having been written as the published books with which we are familiar. Some devotional classics began very differently from that—as letters, for example, or recorded conversations, or scrapbook-like remains brought together posthumously. Additionally, some classics consist partly of the life story surrounding the author. All of these traits apply to *The Practice of the Presence of God* by Brother Lawrence.

Brother Lawrence (1610–1691) was born as Nicholas Herman. In mid-life he entered a monastery in Paris as a lay monk. The legend surrounding Brother Lawrence is even more famous than his treatise. He is the cheerful monk who experienced God's moment-by-moment presence as he washed the pots and pans in the monastery kitchen. A certain unreality and naivete easily seep into the legend. But what did Brother Lawrence actually say in the letters of instruction he wrote to his fellow monks, who naturally wanted to know the secret of his spirituality?

Certainly some of the comments in *The Practice of the Presence of God* set forth an ideal that cannot be literally practiced in our daily routine, but as is true of most of the entries in this anthology, what the author wrote contains an element of surprise when compared to what we *think* we know. We should look for two themes in the passage excerpted from one of Brother Lawrence's letters.

One is that Brother Lawrence does, indeed, call us to a high standard of keeping God in our conscious thoughts as we go about our work and leisure in the world. We should welcome this encouragement to raise the bar higher than we usually do. But the other theme is the realistic one of practicing the presence of God in small ways. What Brother Lawrence instructs us to do is practical. We can be encouraged by what we read because it is within the reach of any true follower of God.

The rhetoric or persuasion in Brother Lawrence's treatise is a brilliant balancing act between, on the one hand, not raising the bar so high that we cannot reach it, and, on the other hand, not dropping the bar so low that we become complacent about our current level of spiritual closeness to God. The excerpted passage moves like a pendulum between the extremes of too much and too little.

—❦—

Brother Lawrence is correctly fixed in the popular imagination with pots and pans in the kitchen. Practicing the presence of God there made the utensils holy. A Bible passage that corresponds to this picture is the golden-age prophecy in Zechariah 14: "And on that day there shall be inscribed on the bells of the horses, 'Holy to the LORD.*' . . . And every pot in Jerusalem and Judah shall be holy to the* LORD *of hosts" (vv. 20–21).*

18

The Saints' Everlasting Rest

RICHARD BAXTER

The very reason why you . . . desire to live on earth is chiefly this, that you may seek the Lord, and make sure of your [heavenly] rest. Though you do not seek it so zealously as you should, yet it is the chief of your desires and endeavors, so that nothing else is desired or preferred before it. You will think no labor or suffering too great to obtain it. And though the flesh may sometimes shrink, yet you are resolved and contented to go through all. Your esteem for it will also be so high, and your affections to it so great, that you would not exchange your title to it, and hopes of it, for any worldly good whatsoever. . . .

Compare the joys which you shall have above with those foretastes of it which the Spirit hath given you here. Has not God sometimes revealed himself extraordinarily to your soul, and let a drop of glory fall upon it? Have you not been ready to say, "O that it might be thus with my soul continually?" . . . Think with yourself, "What is this earnest to the full inheritance? Alas, all this light, that so amazes and rejoices me, is but a candle lighted from heaven, to lead me thither through this world of darkness. . . ."

To see a family live in love, husband and wife, parents, children, and servants, doing all in love to one another; to see a town live together in love, without any envyings, brawlings or contentions, law-suits, factions, or divisions, but every man loving his neighbor as himself, thinking they can never do too much for one another, but striving to go beyond each other in love; how happy, how delightful a sight is this! O then, what a blessed society will the family of heaven be, and those peaceful inhabitants of the New Jerusalem, where there is no division, nor differing judgments, no disaffection nor strangeness, no deceitful friendship, no, not one unkind expression, nor any angry look or thought; but *all are one in Christ*, who is one with the Father, and all live in the love of him, who is love itself! . . .

I hope you will value this heavenly life, and take one walk every day in the new Jerusalem. God is your love, and your desire; you would fain be more acquainted with your Savior; and I know it is your grief that your hearts are not nearer to him, and that they do not more feelingly love him, and delight in him. O try this life of meditation on your heavenly rest! Here is the mount on which the fluctuating ark of your souls may rest. Let the world see by your heavenly lives that religion is something more than opinions and disputes, or a task of outward duties. . . .

As Moses, before he died, went up unto mount Nebo, to take a survey of the land of Canaan; so the Christian ascends this mount of contemplation, and by faith surveys his rest. . . . Thus, as Daniel, in his captivity, daily opened his window toward Jerusalem, though far out of sight, when he went to God in his devotions; so may the believing soul, in this captivity of the flesh, look towards *Jerusalem which is above*.[1]

C. S. Lewis was of the opinion that "a continual looking forward to the eternal world is . . . one of the things a Christian is meant to do."[2] That is the principle that the Puritan Richard Baxter (1645–1691) unfolds at book length in his devotional classic *The Saints' Everlasting Rest*. Baxter covers all of the important facets of heavenly rest—its nature, its glory, the qualifications that entitle a person to it, the impediments to attaining it, and the need to engage in what Baxter calls heavenly contemplation as a way of deriving strength for daily living.

The subject of the passage printed here is heavenly contemplation—how to engage in it and the benefits that flow from it. A firm logic is at work in the successive paragraphs. The first paragraph prompts us to an awareness of the supreme value that we place on heavenly rest. This is the impetus that propels us to contemplate that rest in our devotional life.

The next two paragraphs use the time-honored technique of moving from the lesser to the greater. First Baxter gets us to recall moments of God's visitations to us and the delight we feel when we see a harmonious family and community. Then he pushes us to imagine the time when the moments of visitation will be forever and the redeemed will live in even greater harmony than we see now.

In effect, the first three paragraphs have led us to actually engage in the desired heavenly contemplation. In the two concluding paragraphs, Baxter addresses us directly as a spiritual mentor and encourages us to make heavenly contemplation a daily reality in our spiritual walk.

Baxter possesses a lively poetic imagination. To engage in heavenly contemplation is to take a metaphoric daily walk in the new Jerusalem. When we contemplate heaven, we become a latter-day Moses viewing the promised land from Mount Nebo and, like Daniel, praying toward Jerusalem.

Baxter makes it clear at the outset of his book that the point of departure and moving spirit behind his book is Hebrews 4:9 and 11: "So then, there remains a Sabbath rest for the people of God. . . . Let us therefore strive to enter that rest."

19

What Makes the Bible
the Greatest Book

SAMUEL TAYLOR COLERIDGE

Christianity is fact no less than truth. It is spiritual, yet so as to be historical; and between these two poles there must likewise be a midpoint, in which the historical and spiritual meet. . . . This is a providence, a preparation, and a looking forward to Christ. . . . The sky of my belief is serene, unclouded by a doubt. . . .

I take up [the Bible] with the purpose to read it . . . as I should read any other work, as far at least as I can or dare. For I neither can, nor dare, throw off a strong and awful prepossession in its favor—certain as I am that a large part of the light and life, in and by which I see, love, and embrace the truths and the strengths co-organized into a living body of faith and knowledge . . . is directly or indirectly derived to me from this sacred volume. . . .

[In the Bible] I have met everywhere more or less copious sources of truth, and power, and purifying impulses, have found words for my inmost thoughts, songs for my joy, utterances for my hidden griefs, and pleadings for my shame and my feebleness. In short, whatever *finds* me, bears witness for itself that it has proceeded from a Holy Spirit, even from the same Spirit, *which remaining in itself, yet regenerateth all other powers, and in all ages entering into holy souls, maketh them friends of God, and prophets. . . .*

In the Bible there is more that *finds* me than I have experienced in all other books put together; the words of the Bible find me at greater depths of my being; and whatever finds me brings with it an irresistible evidence of its having proceeded from the Holy Spirit. But the doctrine in question requires me to believe that not only what finds me, but that all that exists in the sacred volume, and which I am bound to find therein, was not alone inspired by, that is composed by, men under the actuating influence of the Holy Spirit, but likewise dictated by an Infallible Intelligence; that the writers, each and all, were divinely informed as well as inspired. Here all evasion, all excuse, is cut off. An infallible intelligence extends to all things, physical no less than spiritual.[1]

***

It is always uplifting and pleasurable to discover that someone of stature whom we did not know to be a person of Christian conviction turns out to be a kindred spirit. Poet Samuel Taylor Coleridge (1772–1834) is a major English poet. His poetry is more Romantic in orientation than Christian, but his best-known masterpiece, *The Rime of the Ancient Mariner*, is a Christian classic, tracing the arc of an original innocence that is lost through a great crime that produces devastating guilt, which is reversed in a moment of forgiveness leading to life restored.

Additionally, there is a little-known side to Coleridge's life and place in Christian thought, and it has to do with his career as a Christian apologist. In turn, an important part of Coleridge's apologetic career is his defense of the Bible. The passage excerpted here is important to us because of what it says about the Bible's distinctiveness, and the fact that the statement comes from an unexpected source is simply a bonus. The key document for Coleridge's view of Scripture is his treatise *Confessions of an Inquiring Spirit*, written late in Coleridge's life and published six years after his death. As the passage hints, it is a kind of spiritual last testament, expressing what Coleridge confesses.

In keeping with the format of "an inquiring spirit," the passage is structured on a stream-of-consciousness principle, with the author sharing his randomly organized thoughts about the Bible. Surely the greatest contribution that Coleridge makes to our understanding of what makes the Bible the greatest book is his insight that the Bible *finds* us at the deepest level of our being. We receive this insight from Coleridge as a revelation, leading us to think, "Yes—that's it. That's what makes the Bible more profound than other books." The superior power of the Bible is that it impacts us in a way that surpasses other books.

Once this inner witness has been established as the core idea, certain external facts about the Bible fill out the picture. The Bible is inspired and authoritative. It bears the imprint of the Holy Spirit and is unified by a Christological focus. Although we might set out to analyze the Bible using the same methods as we apply to other books, we cannot really approach the Bible objectively in that way because of all that is part of our experience of it. All of these insights form a moving testimony about the Book of books, prompting us to think about how each of Coleridge's claims has been true in our own lives.

Coleridge's theme is the superior impact of the Bible on believing readers. This is also the viewpoint of Hebrews 4:12: "For the word of God is living and active, sharper than any two-edged sword, piercing to the division of soul and of spirit, of joints and of marrow, and discerning the thoughts and intentions of the heart."

20

Holy Living

JEREMY TAYLOR

That God is present in all places, that he sees every action, hears all discourses and understands every thought, is no strange thing to a Christian ear who hath been taught this doctrine. . . . We may imagine God to be as the air and the sea, and we all enclosed in his circle, wrapped up in the lap of his infinite nature; or as infants in the wombs of their pregnant mothers: and we can no more be removed from the presence of God than from our own being. . . .

God is especially present in the hearts of his people by his Holy Spirit; and indeed the hearts of holy men are temples. . . . For God reigns in the hearts of his servants; there is his kingdom. . . . The temple itself is the heart of man; Christ is the high-priest, who from thence sends up the incense of prayers, and joins them to his own intercession, and presents all together to his Father; and the Holy Spirit, by his dwelling there, hath also consecrated it into a temple; and God dwells in our hearts by faith and Christ by his Spirit, and the Spirit by his purities: so that we are also cabinets of the mysterious Trinity; and what is this short of heaven itself, but as infancy is short of manhood. . . .

Now the consideration of this great truth is of a very universal use in the whole course of the life of a Christian. . . . He that remembers that God stands a witness and a judge, beholding every secrecy, besides his impiety, must have put on impudence, if he be not much restrained in his temptation to sin. For the greatest part of sin is taken away if a man have a witness of his conversation. . . . [God] is to be feared in public; he is to be feared in private: if you go forth, he spies you; if you go in, he sees you: when you light the candle, he observes you; when you put it out, then also God marks you. Be sure, that while you are in his sight, you behave yourself as becomes so holy a presence. . . .

And this [can be] called a building to God a chapel in our heart. It reconciles Martha's employment with Mary's devotion, charity, and religion; the necessities of our calling, and the employments of devotion. For thus in the midst of the works of your trade, you may retire into your chapel [your heart] and converse with God by frequent addresses and returns. . . .

Let us remember that God is in us, and that we are in him; we are his workmanship; let us not deface it: we are in his presence; let us not pollute it by unholy and impure actions. . . . God is in every place; suppose it therefore to be a church. . . .

He walks as in the presence of God, that converses with him in frequent prayer and frequent communion, that runs to him in all his necessities, that asks counsel of him in all his doubtings, that opens all his wants to him, that weeps before him for his sins. . . . [1]

Jeremy Taylor (1613–1667), a seventeenth-century Anglican clergyman, is known to posterity for his book commonly known as *Holy Living and Holy Dying*. This is actually the collective title of two devotional books published a year apart (1650 and 1651). *Holy Living* is a guide to the virtuous life and is an encyclopedic discussion of morality and piety, accompanied by directives, prayers, and exercises. Some devotional writers (including ones in this anthology) discuss *holiness*, which leads to an exploration of character or *being* holy; Taylor puts the emphasis on *holy living*, which leads to a description of action and lifestyle.

In his book, before Taylor gets to the subject of individual moral virtues, he lays out the foundational principle of holy living. In his view, the way to live a holy life is to live every waking minute in an awareness that we are in the presence of God. As he elaborates this core idea in the passage printed here, we cannot help but agree that if we are aware of living in the presence of God, we have the strongest possible incentive to do what is right and avoid what is sinful.

In addition to the winsome simplicity and impeccable logic of this foundational premise, the passage sparkles with Taylor's metaphoric imagination, as he uses various spheres of life to shed light on the central topic of holy living. Thus our heart or soul is variously a *temple* in which the triune God ministers, a *kingdom* in which God rules, and a *chapel* to which we retire to meet with God. Since God is everywhere, the whole world is a *church*. And so forth.

In the background of Taylor's thinking is 1 Corinthians 3:16–17: "Do you not know that you are God's temple and that God's Spirit dwells in you? . . . God's temple is holy, and you are that temple."

21

Earthly and Divine Beauty

JONATHAN EDWARDS

When we are delighted with flowery meadows and gentle breezes of wind, we may consider that we see only the emanations of the sweet benevolence of Jesus Christ. When we behold the fragrant rose and lily, we see His love and purity. So the green trees and fields and singing of birds are the emanations of His infinite joy and benignity [kindness]. The easiness and naturalness of trees and vines are shadows of His beauty and loveliness. The crystal rivers and murmuring streams are the footsteps of His favor, grace, and beauty. When we behold the light and brightness of the sun, the golden edges of an evening cloud, or the beauteous rainbow, we behold the adumbrations of His glory and goodness; and in the blue sky of His mildness and gentleness.

There are also many things wherein we may behold His awful majesty, in the sun in his strength, in comets, in thunder, in the hovering thunder-clouds, in ragged rocks, and the brows of mountains. That beauteous light with which the world is filled in a clear day, is a lively shadow of His spotless holiness, and happiness and delight in communicating Himself. . . .

For as God is infinitely the greatest Being, so he is allowed to be infinitely the most beautiful and excellent: and all the beauty to be found throughout the whole creation, is but the reflection of the diffused beams of that Being who has an infinite fullness of brightness and glory. God's beauty is infinitely more valuable than that of all other beings upon both those accounts mentioned, namely, the degree of his virtue, and the greatness of his being, possessed of this virtue.

Because God is not only infinitely greater and more excellent than all other being, but he is the head of the universal system of existence; the foundation and fountain of all being and all beauty; from whom all is perfectly derived, and on whom all is most absolutely and perfectly dependent; of whom, and through whom, and to whom is all being and all perfection; and whose being and beauty are, as it were, the sum and comprehension of all existence and excellence: much more than the sun is the fountain and summary comprehension of all the light and brightness of the day. . . .

Fully to enjoy God, is infinitely better than the most pleasant accommodations here. Better than fathers and mothers, husbands, wives or children, or the company of any, or all earthly friends. These are but shadows; but the enjoyment of God is the substance. These are but scattered beams; but God is the sun. These are but streams; but God is the fountain. These are but drops; but God is the ocean.[1]

Jonathan Edwards (1703–1758) was a New England preacher, theologian, and philosopher in the Puritan tradition. The common image of Edwards is that he was a stern Calvinist. Those who have read widely in his writings, and even more, scholars who have studied his thought in depth, view Edwards in quite a different light. In the annals of great theologians, Edwards based more of his religious thought on the concept of beauty than anyone else. The entry printed here is a devotional meditation on earthly and divine beauty, and the relationship between them. Edwards invites us to think about beauty on three levels.

One is the earthly beauty that we see around us in nature and the arts. Edwards does not *tell* us that we are surrounded by beauty but instead *shows* us by his rapturous descriptive vocabulary and power of observation. The descriptive touches in Edwards's prose are what literary scholars call prose poetry. The application we can make of Edwards's words is to resolve to take note of the beauty that is making itself available all around us.

Once we are moved by beauty in this way, we are naturally led to wonder where it comes from and how we can be appropriately grateful for the gift. The passage repeatedly asserts that God is the source of all beauty, but that assertion by itself is a platitude. Edwards takes the subject to a whole new level with his imagery of earthly beauty being an emanation from God as its source. This does more than make God the source of beauty. It opens the door to seeing all of our experiences of beauty as a means of apprehending God in his being at the present moment. When we see beauty, we are seeing God.

Then thirdly, Edwards turns all of this admirable thinking about beauty and God in a doxological direction. In fact, the point that comes to dominate the excerpt is the supremacy of God over everything else. Our imaginations and spirits soar as the passage finds ever-new ways to exalt God, who is celebrated as being paradoxically both transcendent (above creation) and immanent (present in creation).

Edwards is known primarily as a preacher, theologian, and philosopher, but this passage shows him to be a poet. The passage gains its impact by means of its marvelous imagery and metaphors. These are what lead us to *feel* the supremacy of God, as he is declared to be the *sun* that produces the *scattered beams* of light, and the *ocean* compared to water *drops*.

Edwards's exaltation of the supremacy of God brings the Christ hymn of Colossians 1 to mind. Here is an excerpt: "By him all things were created, in heaven and on earth. . . . He is before all things, and in him all things hold together. . . . He is the beginning, the firstborn from the dead, that in everything he might be preeminent" (vv. 16–18).

22

Morning Prayer

BOOK OF COMMON PRAYER

The Scripture moveth us, in sundry places,
to acknowledge and confess our manifold sins and wickedness;
and that we should not dissemble nor cloak them
before the face of Almighty God our heavenly Father;
but confess them with an humble, lowly, penitent, and obedient
   heart;
to the end that we may obtain forgiveness of the same,
by his infinite goodness and mercy.

Almighty and most merciful Father,
we have erred and strayed from thy ways like lost sheep.
We have followed too much the devices and desires of our own
   hearts.
We have offended against thy holy laws.
We have left undone those things which we ought to have done;
And we have done those things which we ought not to have
   done;
And there is no health in us.

But thou, O Lord, have mercy upon us, miserable offenders.
Spare thou those, O God, who confess their faults.
Restore thou those who are penitent;

According to thy promises declared unto mankind in Christ
  Jesus our Lord.
And grant, O most merciful Father, for his sake,
That we may hereafter live a godly, righteous, and sober life,
To the glory of thy holy Name. Amen.

Almighty God, the Father of our Lord Jesus Christ,
who desireth not the death of a sinner,
but rather that he may turn from his wickedness and live, . . .
[who] pardoneth and absolveth all those who truly repent
and unfeignedly believe his holy Gospel, . . .
grant us true repentance and his Holy Spirit,
that those things may please him which we do at this present;
and that the rest of our life hereafter may be pure and holy;
so that at the last we may come to his eternal joy;
through Jesus Christ our Lord. . . .

We praise thee,
we bless thee,
we worship thee,
we glorify thee,
we give thanks to thee for thy great glory,
O Lord God heavenly King, God the Father Almighty.[1]

The first thing to be noted is that this prayer is phrased in such a way as to fit its intended context of public worship. This need not deter us from assimilating it as a private devotional. One way to do this is to imagine ourselves present at a corporate meeting with fellow Christians. The other is to allow the plural references to *we* and *us* serve as a reminder that whenever we pray or contemplate Christian truth in a devotional, we are part of the church universal. Praying in the plural can be a salutary reminder of that fact.

What makes the morning prayer from the Prayer Book so elevating and memorable? The language and style, first of all. The verbal beauty of the prayer has made some of the phrases part of the cultural consciousness through the centuries, even in non-Anglican circles. The archaic language lends an appropriate dignity and sense of tradition to the prayer. Elegant epithets (titles for a person or thing) are always a feature of the grand style, and they are an important part of the effect here—epithets like *Almighty God our heavenly Father* and *the Father of our Lord Jesus Christ*. The Greek playwright Aristophanes said that "high thoughts must have high language."[2] Anyone who doubts that God approves of eloquent and rhetorically embellished prayers should read Solomon's prayer at the dedication of the temple (2 Chronicles 6) to allay their doubts.

The primary subject matter of this prayerful meditation is the confession and forgiveness of sin. This is the great priority in life, and it is always good to renew our commitment to this truth. Praying this prayer shows us how to be a true penitent. But the prayer has many other dimensions of the Christian faith radiating outward from the core of sin and forgiveness. As we claim the thoughts of the prayer for ourselves, we commit ourselves to live *a godly, righteous, and sober life*. We also contemplate how *at the last we may come to* [God's] *eternal joy*. Overshadowing the whole prayer is a pervasive praise of God for his greatness.

Everything about the prayer elevates—elevates God, elevates us to a high spiritual level even in the act of confessing our sins, elevates religious language. We finish this exalted meditation feeling purified and energized to live for God. We feel that we have been in the presence of something great.

The motions of the soul that are enshrined in the morning prayer of the Prayer Book are paralleled by Psalm 143:8:

> *Let me hear in the morning of your steadfast love,*
> *for in you I trust.*
> *Make me know the way I should go,*
> *for to you I lift up my soul.*

23

Reflections on the Supreme Loveliness of Christ

FYODOR DOSTOYEVSKY, JONATHAN EDWARDS,

AND THOMAS WATSON

God gives me sometimes moments of perfect peace; in such moments I love and believe that I am loved; in such moments I have formulated my creed, wherein all is clear and holy to me. This creed is extremely simple; here it is: I believe that there is nothing lovelier, deeper, more sympathetic, more rational, more manly, and more perfect than the Savior; I say to myself with jealous love that not only is there no one else like Him, but that there could be no one.[1]

Fyodor Dostoyevsky (1821–1881)

I have loved the doctrines of the gospel; they have been to my soul like green pastures. The gospel has seemed to me the richest treasure; the treasure that I have most desired, and longed that it might dwell richly in me. The way of salvation by Christ has appeared, in a general way, glorious and excellent, most pleasant and most beautiful. It has often seemed to me, that it would, in a great measure, spoil heaven, to receive it in any other way. . . .

It has often appeared to me delightful to be united to Christ; to have him for my Head, and to be a member of his body; also to have Christ for my Teacher and Prophet. I very often think with sweetness, and longings, and pantings of soul, of being a little child, taking hold of Christ, to be led by him through the wilderness of this world. . . . I love to think of coming to Christ, to receive salvation of him, poor in spirit, and quite empty of self, humbly exalting him alone; cut off entirely from my own root, in order to grow into, and out of Christ; to have God in Christ to be all in all; and to live by faith on the Son of God, a life of humble, unfeigned confidence in him.[2]

Jonathan Edwards (1703–1758)

Christ is our light. . . . This Sun of Righteousness is more glorious than the sun in the sky. The sun in the firmament rises and sets—but the Sun of Righteousness, once it rises upon the soul in conversion, never sets finally upon him. . . . The sun in the sky only shines *upon* us—but the Sun of Righteousness shines *within* us. . . . The sun in the sky shines only upon our faces—but the Sun of Righteousness shines in our hearts. . . . And how sweet are these beams! . . . Oh, how lovely in this Sun of Righteousness! By the bright beams of this Sun, we see God. . . .

Christ must be dearer to us than all. He must weigh heavier than relations in the balance of our affections. . . . Christ's *gleanings* are better than the world's *vintage*. . . . If Christ is so lovely in Himself, then you who profess Christ, labor to render Him lovely in the eyes of others.[3]

Thomas Watson (1620–1686)

———— ✠ ————

The ultimate purpose of devotional writing is to awaken and express our love for God. This medley of excerpts (one from a world-famous Russian novelist and two from Puritan ministers) focuses our affection on a single member of the Trinity.

The genre of the three selections is known as *panegyric*—a composition that praises a person or thing in superlative terms. A panegyric, moreover, has the quality of a public declaration. It accordingly possesses a dignity of expression in which we receive the impression that the words and sentiments have been very carefully chosen for posterity. The three selections fit this pattern. Dostoyevsky calls his statement a creed. The passage from Jonathan Edwards is a climactic passage in his spiritual autobiography titled *A Personal Narrative*. And Thomas Watson's Christocentric rhapsody is an excerpt from a sermon titled "The Loveliness of Christ."

The rhetoric of a panegyric can be summarized under the formula "the search for superlatives." Nearly everything in the three passages illustrates this, with a vocabulary of *more* and *most* and *richest* and *dearer* and *better* and such like. The effect is to elevate Christ above everything else.

The poetic impulse also permeates the passages. Edwards pictures coming to Christ for salvation as a child taking hold of Christ and being led by him, and as a plant having its roots cut off and being grafted into Christ. Watson devotes a whole paragraph to unfolding the metaphoric dimensions of Christ as our *Sun*. His musing on the mere gleanings of Christ being better than the best offerings of the world is a clever allusion to Gideon's calming the anger of the men of Ephraim for not having been summoned to defeat the Midianites (Judg. 8:2).

We need to add a famous statement by the renowned British Victorian poet Alfred, Lord Tennyson to our gallery. Once when Tennyson was walking with a visitor in a garden, the visitor asked the poet what he thought of Christ. After pausing for a minute, Tennyson replied, "What the sun is to that flower, Jesus Christ is to my soul. He is the sun of my soul."[4]

The supremacy of Christ finds memorable expression in the Christ hymn of Colossians 1:15–20. In the middle of the passage we read this: "He is the beginning, the firstborn from the dead, that in everything he might be preeminent. For in him all the fullness of God was pleased to dwell" (vv. 18–19).

24

On Loving God

BERNARD OF CLAIRVAUX

The reason for loving God is God Himself. . . . Could any [reason] be greater than this, that He gave Himself for us unworthy wretches? And being God, what better gift could He offer than Himself? Hence, if one seeks for God's claim upon our love, here is the chiefest: because He first loved us (1 John 4:19). Ought He not to be loved in return, when we think who loved, whom He loved, and how much He loved? . . . Our love is not a gift but a debt. And since it is the Godhead who loves us, Himself boundless, eternal, supreme love, of whose greatness there is no end, . . . can we think of repaying Him grudgingly? . . .

And now let us consider what profit we shall have from loving God. . . . There is a double reason constraining us: His right and our advantage. . . . Although God would be loved without respect of reward, yet He wills not to leave love unrewarded. . . . Love is an affection of the soul, not a contract. . . . It is spontaneous in its origin and impulse; and true love is its own satisfaction. It has its reward, but that reward is the object beloved. . . .

Praise the Lord, O my soul,
who satisfies thy mouth with good things.
He bestows bounty immeasurable;
He provokes thee to good;
He preserves thee in goodness;

He comes before, He sustains, He fills thee;
He moves thee to longing;
and it is He for whom you long.

I have said already that the motive for loving God is God Himself. And I spoke truly, for He is as well the efficient cause as the
final object of our love.

He gives the occasion for love;
He creates the affection;
He brings the desire to good effect.

Our love is prepared and rewarded by His. He loves us first, out
of His great tenderness; then we are bound to repay Him with
love; and we are permitted to cherish exultant hopes in Him.
"He is rich unto all that call upon Him" (Rom. 10:12), yet He
has no gift for them better than Himself.

He gives Himself as prize and reward;
He is the refreshment of the holy soul,
the ransom of those in captivity.
"The Lord is good unto them that wait for Him" (Lam. 3:25).

What will He be then to those who gain His presence? But here
is a paradox, that no one can seek the Lord who has not already
found Him. It is Thy will, O God, to be found that Thou mayest be
sought, to be sought that Thou mayest the more truly be found.[1]

Bernard of Clairvaux (1090–1154) was a French monk living in the
high Middle Ages. He is best known for his hymns "Jesus, Thou Joy
of Loving Hearts" and "Jesus, the Very Thought of Thee." He is also
famous for a devotional classic titled *On Loving God*, from which the
passage here is taken. Bernard composed the work in response to a
request from a cardinal in Rome who had asked why we should love
God and in what measure. Bernard's short answer, stated in the second
sentence of his entire treatise (not the devotional passage printed here,

which is from later in his treatise), is that our motive for loving God is God himself, and the quantity of love due to God is without measure.

The key to navigating Bernard's treatise is to accept that it is structured on a principle known as stream of consciousness. This means it follows the thought process of the author instead of being organized by paragraphs with topic sentences forming a logical flow. Stream of consciousness is a common strategy in devotional writing because it gives us not just the product of the author's thought but the process of thinking, which lends a meditative cast to the writing.

The excerpted passage epitomizes the content of Bernard's treatise. Its subject is loving God, and as the author meditates on that subject, two main ideas emerge, namely, the duty we have to love God, and the advantages that come to us as a reward for loving God. These two motifs are woven together in the excerpted passage, and looking for them is a good analytic template as we live with the passage.

All of the devotional classics that make up this anthology rise above the level of straightforward expository prose. They do not carry all of their meaning on the surface but require unpacking. The intermixture of topics noted here is one of these techniques. Some parts of the passage employ parallelism of clauses, and they have been printed as verse to highlight the element of artistry and verbal beauty. These interspersed passages of praise of God for his generous acts embody the very principle that Bernard asserts—that God deserves our love.

Additionally, Bernard employs a rhetoric of paradox that yields fresh insights as we wrestle with his statements. For example, loving God is itself a reward. We seek God because we have already found him. God wants us to find him so we will seek him. *How can such things be?* we wonder. As we pursue our puzzlement, things begin to make sense while yet retaining an appropriate quality of mystery.

The central idea of Bernard's treatise is encapsulated in Jesus's words recorded in Matthew 22:37–38: "You shall love the Lord your God with all your heart and with all your soul and with all your mind. This is the great and first commandment."

25

The Rare Jewel of Christian Contentment

Jeremiah Burroughs

Spiritual contentment comes from the frame of the soul. The contentment of a man or woman who is rightly content does not come so much from outward arguments or from any outward help, as from the disposition of their own hearts. The disposition of their own hearts causes and brings forth this gracious contentment rather than any external thing. . . . I would unfold this to you with this simile: to be content as a result of some external thing is like warming a man's clothes by the fire. But to be content through an inward disposition of the soul is like the warmth that a man's clothes have from the natural heat of the body. A man who is healthy in body puts on his clothes, and perhaps at first on a cold morning they feel cold. But after he has had them on a little while they are warm. How did they get warm? [Because] they were near the fire? No, this came from the natural heat of his body. . . . The warmth of the fire, that is, a contentment that results merely from external arguments, will not last long. But that which comes from the gracious temper of one's spirit will last. . . .

By contentment, we come to give God the worship that is His due. It is a special part of the divine worship that we owe to God to be content in a Christian way. You worship God more by this than when you come to hear a sermon or spend an hour in prayer. These are acts of God's worship, but they are only external acts of worship. But this is the soul's worship: to subject itself thus to God. You who often will worship God by hearing and praying, and yet afterwards will be discontented—know that God . . . will [rather] have the soul's worship, the subjecting of the soul unto God. In active obedience, we worship God by doing what pleases God; but by passive obedience, we do as well worship God by being pleased with what God does. . . .

All the rules and helps in the world will do us little good unless we get a good temper within our hearts. You can never make a ship go steady by propping it outside; you know there must be ballast within the ship to make it go steady. So there is nothing outside us that can keep our hearts in a steady, constant way, but grace within the soul. . . . Exercise much faith: that is the way for contentedness. . . . Exercise faith by often resigning yourself to God, by giving yourself up to God and His ways. The more you surrender up yourself to God in a believing way, the more peace and quiet you will have. Labor to be spiritually minded. That is, be often in meditation of the things that are above. "If ye then be risen with Christ, seek those things which are above, where Christ sitteth on the right hand of God" (Col. 3:1). . . . [1]

Jeremiah Burroughs (1599–1646) was a prominent Puritan preacher and even a member of the Westminster Assembly at the very time the Puritans were gaining ascendancy in England. Like many entries in this anthology, the title of Burroughs's best-known book—*The Rare Jewel of Christian Contentment*—is so thought provoking that it is a mini-devotional all by itself.

The title catches our attention first of all by putting the Christian virtue of *contentment* on our agenda of thinking. Most Christians feel convicted by this because they know that contentment is one of the most difficult virtues to achieve in our own culture. As we ponder the title further, it dawns on us that *Christian* contentment is different from a merely human bent of temperament. Then by introducing the metaphor of a *jewel*, Burroughs implicitly asserts that Christian contentment is beautiful and something to be treasured. The final stroke is to call Christian contentment a *rare* jewel, with the multiple meanings of something infrequently attained and therefore very highly prized and of extreme value.

In typical Puritan fashion, Burroughs gives his topic the complete treatment in his book, dividing it into a negative half and a positive half. The negative aspect takes the form of an analysis of the evil of discontent, or murmuring against God's providence when adversity comes. The excerpts printed here epitomize the positive message.

The first paragraph is a summary of the section of the book in which Burroughs defines the nature of Christian contentment. It is not a cheerful temperament arising from external comforts, but an inner spiritual quality. The second paragraph comes from the section devoted to the excellence of contentment, and the original slant on that subject is that Christian contentment is an act of worship. The third paragraph comes from the section on how to attain contentment, and the emphasis is on the exercise of faith in all that we believe about God's goodness and the primacy of the spiritual.

Burroughs believes that Christian contentment is not innate in human nature but something to be learned. In fact, he devotes a whole section to the subject of "how Christ teaches contentment." A constant point of reference throughout Burroughs's treatise is Paul's claim in Philippians 4:11: "For I have learned, in whatsoever state I am, therewith to be content" (KJV).

26

Nature as God's Signpost

Nathaniel Hawthorne

I went out to walk about an hour ago, and found it very pleasant. . . . I went round and across the Common, and stood on the highest point of it, where I could see miles and miles into the country. Blessed be God for this green tract, and the view which it affords, whereby we poor citizens may be put in mind that all his earth is not composed of blocks of brick houses, and of stone or wooden pavements. Blessed be God for the sky, too. . . .

Life now swells and heaves beneath me like a brimful ocean; and the endeavor to comprise any portion of it in words is like trying to dip up the ocean in a goblet. . . . God bless and keep us! For there is something more awful [awe-inspiring] in happiness than in sorrow, the latter being earthly and finite, the former composed of the substance and texture of eternity, so that spirits still embodied may tremble at it. . . .

This is a glorious day—bright, very warm, yet with an unspeakable gentleness both in its warmth and brightness. On such days it is impossible not to love Nature, for she evidently loves us. At other seasons she does not give me this impression, or only at very rare intervals; but in these happy, autumnal days, when she has perfected the harvests, and accomplished every necessary thing that she had to do, she overflows with a blessed superfluity of love. It is good to be alive now. Thank God for breath—yes, for mere breath!—when it is made up of such a heavenly breeze as this. It comes to the cheek with a real kiss; it would linger fondly around us, if it might; but, since it must be gone, it caresses us with its whole kindly heart, to caress likewise the next thing it meets. There is a pervading blessing diffused over all the world. I look out of the window and think, "O perfect day! O beautiful world! O good God!" And such a day is the promise of a blissful eternity. Our Creator would never have made such weather, and given us the deep heart to enjoy it, above and beyond all thought, if he had not meant us to be immortal. It opens the gates of heaven and gives us glimpses far inward.[1]

Nathaniel Hawthorne (1804–1864) was not part of the churchgoing public of his day, but what he wrote is Christian in allegiance. His signature work of fiction, *The Scarlet Letter*, is a Christian classic. The climax of that story, the protagonist's confession of sin and acceptance of God's forgiveness, follows all of the steps in the order of salvation as presented in the Bible and codified by Puritan doctrine. Hawthorne's notebooks (from which the excerpts here are taken) are filled with references to God, leading a literary critic to say that Hawthorne was "innately religious" and "more than any other writer of his time . . . a God-centered man."[2]

Many devotional writers prompt us to an awareness of God's presence in nature, but Hawthorne goes beyond this conventional theme in multiple ways. We can note first the undertow of rapture in Hawthorne's words, as his emotional response keeps breaking out in exclamation and poetic expression. These exclamations consistently turn the focus from nature to God. They remind us of certain touches in the Psalms, including doxological statements that God is to be blessed, and expressions of thanks to God for his gifts in nature.

Going beyond these conventions of God-centered nature writing, Hawthorne then insists that the perfection and beauty of earthly nature bear a real relationship to heavenly perfection. Nature assures us of an eternal world and gives us a foreshadowing of it. Throughout the passage, Hawthorne leads us to see that nature is God's signpost, both to himself and to the eternal world that awaits us. There is much in Hawthorne's words that expresses what we too see and feel in nature, and additionally Hawthorne leads us to see more in nature than we ordinarily do.

Hawthorne's reflections on nature and his lyric responses to it invite comparison with the nature poems in the book of Psalms. Psalm 8:1 is a parallel that extols God as being glorious both in nature and in an eternal world beyond nature:

> O LORD, our Lord,
>> *how majestic is your name in all the earth!*
> *You have set your glory above the heavens.*

27

Thoughts on the Mission and Greatness of Jesus

BLAISE PASCAL

Jesus Christ is the goal of all, and the center to which all tends. Who knows him knows the reason of all things. . . . All who seek God apart from Jesus Christ, and who rest in nature, either find no light to satisfy them, or form for themselves a means of knowing God and serving him without a mediator. . . . Not only do we know God by Jesus Christ alone, but we know ourselves by Jesus Christ alone. We know life and death by Jesus Christ alone. Apart from Jesus Christ we know not what is our life, nor our death, nor God, nor ourselves. . . . Without Jesus Christ, man must be plunged in vice and misery; with Jesus Christ, man is free from vice and misery, in him is all our virtue and all our happiness. . . .

Jesus Christ, without riches, and without any exterior manifestation of science, is in his own order of holiness. He gave forth no scientific inventions to the world, he never reigned; but he was humble, patient, holy; holy before God, terrible to devils, without spot of sin. O! . . . with what transcendent magnificence did he come to the eyes of the heart which discern wisdom. . . . It would have been needless to our Lord Jesus Christ for the purpose of shining in his kingdom of holiness, to come as kings come; but he did come in the glory proper to his order. It is most

unreasonable to be offended at the lowliness of Jesus Christ. . . .
[We should] do little things as though they were great, because
of the majesty of Jesus Christ who does them in us, and who
lives our life; [and] do great things as though they were small
and easy, because of his omnipotence. . . .

I consider Jesus Christ in all persons and in ourselves. Jesus
Christ as a father in his father, Jesus Christ as a brother in his
brethren, Jesus Christ as poor in the poor, Jesus Christ as rich
in the rich, Jesus Christ as doctor and priest in priests, Jesus
Christ as sovereign in princes, etc. For by his glory he is all that
is great, since he is God; and he is by his mortal life all that is
miserable and abject. Therefore he has taken this wretched state,
to enable him to be in all persons, and the model of all condi-
tions. . . . Each day of my life I bless my Redeemer, . . . who has
transformed me, a man full of weakness, misery, and lust, of
pride and ambition, into a man exempt from these evils, by the
power of his grace, to which all the glory is due.[1]

—⊷⊷⊷—

Blaise Pascal (1623–1662) was a famous French mathematician, scientist, inventor, philosopher, theologian, and writer. This combination
makes him a central figure in the intellectual history of the West. He
was above all a thinker. At the age of thirty-one, Pascal experienced an
intense conversion that was so momentous to him that he recorded it
on a piece of paper (now known as the *Memorial*) that he carried with
him daily until his death, transferring it from one garment to another
when he changed clothes. The piece was discovered by a servant after
Pascal's death, sewn into the coat he was wearing at the time of his
death.

Pascal's signature work is titled *Pensées*, meaning "thoughts" or
"reflections." It is a collection of fragments—a scrapbook of hundreds
of bits and pieces—on philosophic and religious subjects. It was intended to be a work of Christian apologetics, or defense of the faith,
but when Pascal died at the age of thirty-nine, the work was only a collection of materials from which an eventual book might be constructed.

With many devotionals that rise above the realm of the ordinary, it is the element of the unexpected, a kind of dissonance, that provides the voltage. Pascal was a towering intellectual, but the passage printed here surprises us by embracing the simplicity of the gospel, the humility of Jesus, and the neediness of people. The unifying theme of the passage is the mission and greatness of Jesus, a heading that appears in the edition from which the material has been taken. The genre of the selection is known as *panegyric*, a piece that praises a person. As we follow Pascal's doxological reflections, he becomes our spokesman, saying what we too feel and want to express as our adoration of Christ. There are original twists to Pascal's thoughts about Jesus as well, worthy of our contemplation.

In some parts of Pensées, *Pascal presents intellectual arguments to prove the truthfulness of the Christian faith, but in the passage that appears here his purpose is to praise rather than prove. The Christ hymns of the New Testament are similar in nature. The following excerpt from the Christ hymn at the beginning of the Gospel of John is an example: "And the Word became flesh and dwelt among us, and we have seen his glory, glory as of the only Son from the Father, full of grace and truth. . . . No one has ever seen God; the only God, who is at the Father's side, he has made him known" (John 1:14, 18).*

28

Holy Dying

JEREMY TAYLOR

He that would die well must always look for death, every day knocking at the gates of the grave, and then the gates of the grave shall never prevail upon him to do him mischief. . . .

He that would die well must all the days of his life lay up against the day of death, not only by the general provisions of holiness and a pious life, but provisions proper to the necessities of that great day . . . in which a man is to throw his last cast for an eternity of joys or sorrows; ever remembering, that this alone well performed is not enough to pass us into Paradise, but that done foolishly is enough to send us to hell; and the want of either a holy life, or death, makes a man to fall short of the mighty price of our high calling. . . .

Men in the course of their lives walk lazily . . . and when they are passively revolved to the time of their dissolution, they have no mercies in store, no patience, no faith, no charity to God, or despite of the world, being without appetite for the land of their inheritance, which Christ with so much pain and blood had purchased for them. When we come to die indeed, . . . we shall find how much we have need to have secured the Spirit of God, and the grace of a habitual, perfect unmovable resolution. . . . God rewards the piety of our lives by his gracious acceptance and benediction, upon the actions preparatory to our deathbed. . . .

He that will die well and happily must dress his soul by a diligent and frequent scrutiny. He must perfectly understand, and watch the state of his soul; he must set his house in order before he be fit to die. . . . Therefore it were but reason we should sum up our accounts at the foot of every page, I mean, that we call ourselves to scrutiny every night when we compose ourselves to the little images of death [i.e., darkness and sleep]. . . . It is not intended that we should take accounts of our lives only to be thought religious, but that we may see our evil and amend it, that we dash our sins against the stones, that we may go to God, and to a spiritual guide, and search for remedies and apply them. . . .

And it will appear highly fitting, if we remember that at the day of judgment, not only the greatest lines of life, but every branch and circumstance of every action, every word and thought shall be called to scrutiny and severe judgment. . . . The way to prevent God's anger is to be angry with ourselves, and by examining our actions and condemning the criminal, by being assessors in God's tribunal. . . . Then Christ's kingdom is set up in our hearts; then we always live in the eye of our Judge, and live by the measures of reason, religion, and sober counsels. . . . [1]

The book for which Jeremy Taylor (1613–1667) is known in the annals of devotional writing, *Holy Living and Holy Dying*, is a bringing together of two books originally published a year apart. Once we have read what Taylor says about holy living, we find ourselves in the position of the proverb about waiting for the second foot to fall, curious about what he says about how to die.

Holy Dying belongs to a voluminous devotional genre dating back to the fifteenth century. Its Latin title is *ars moriendi*—the art of dying. This genre flourished when people lived close to death, and it has dried up in our own day because we are removed from the frequency and physical realities of the process of dying.

How can we die well? Taylor wins us with the simplicity of his answer: we can die well by preparing for our own death. That is the rubric under which we can assimilate the printed passage, as each paragraph adds another thought about how we can prepare for the day of our death.

Taylor's prose is a poetic prose that stands out from ordinary informational prose, especially through its frequent metaphors. Randomly chosen examples from the passage printed here include comparing the process of preparation for death to gathering provisions for a journey, taking time every day to take stock of our spiritual state is like putting on a garment, and coming to the end of our days is like a fisherman casting his line for the last time. Taylor's aphoristic flair sparkles with his observation that *the way to prevent God's anger is to be angry with ourselves.*

⟨⟨⟩⟩

Jeremy Taylor's book-length instruction guide on the subject of preparing for death is an expansion of the prophet Isaiah's directive to King Hezekiah as narrated in 2 Kings 20:1: "Thus says the Lord, *'Set your house in order, for you shall die.'"*

29

Trusting and Praising God in Extremity

William Bradford

Being thus arrived in a good harbor, and brought safe to land, they [the Pilgrims] fell upon their knees and blessed the God of Heaven who had brought them over the vast and furious ocean, and delivered them from all the perils and miseries thereof, again to set their feet on the firm and stable earth, their proper element. . . . Having thus passed the vast ocean, and a sea of troubles before in their preparation . . . , they had now no friends to welcome them nor inns to entertain or refresh their weather-beaten bodies; no houses or much less town to repair to, to seek for help. . . . The season was winter, and they that know the winters of that country know them to be sharp and violent, and subject to cruel and fierce storms, dangerous to travel to known places, much more to search an unknown coast. . . .

For whatever way they turned their eyes (save upward to the heavens), they could have little solace or content in respect of any outward objects. For summer being done, all things stand upon them with a weather-beaten face, and the whole country, full of woods and thickets, represented a wild and savage hue. If they looked behind them, there was the mighty ocean which they had passed and was now as a main bar and gulf to separate them from all the civil parts of the world. . . . Let it also be considered what weak hopes of supply and help they left behind them, that might bear up their minds in this sad condition and trials they were under; and they could not but be very small. . . .

What could now sustain them but the Spirit of God and His grace? May not and ought not the children of these fathers rightly say: "Our fathers were Englishmen which came over this great ocean, and were ready to perish in this wilderness; but they cried unto the Lord, and He heard their voice and looked on their adversity." Let them therefore praise the Lord, because He is good, and His mercies endure forever.[1]

<hr />

This passage is William Bradford's (1590–1657) account of the landing of the Pilgrims at Plymouth Rock, and of his appeal to the struggling group to trust in God and even praise him in their extremity. This entry has been selected for this anthology because of the fame of the passage and the event that it commemorates. An event itself can form the core of a devotional—a real-life, living devotional. The famous story of the Pilgrims' survival in the new world merges with Governor Bradford's moving words, which serve as a commentary on the event.

William Bradford's book *Of Plymouth Plantation* is the official account of the Pilgrims' journey on the *Mayflower* and their settlement in the new world. The passage under consideration is structured on the principle of a crisis and a response. Together these serve a devotional purpose. The crisis that Bradford hints at was extreme. The Pilgrims arrived as winter was setting in. Nearly half of the original hundred died during the first winter. As we ponder this spectacle, we can profitably reflect on our own vulnerability and the circumstances in our lives that we cannot control.

Having shared the extremities that make us kindred spirits with the Pilgrims, we can note the response that Bradford offered to his fellow sufferers and to us. That response is to take refuge in the God of providence and of our salvation. Bradford's appeal has two dimensions. One is to acknowledge that God looks on us in our extremity, bringing us confidence that we can trust God not to abandon us. The second dimension is to praise God for his care.

As Bradford drew his meditation to a close, he quoted the opening verses of Psalm 107. This is small wonder, because later verses in this psalm encapsulate the experience of the Pilgrims, namely, a perilous journey by sea that many times threatened to destroy them, a quest for a safe harbor and place to dwell, and praise of God for his provision. We ourselves do not undertake a literal journey by sea, but the application of this devotional passage is that in our own perilous journey of life, we too can choose to trust God for deliverance and praise him for his provision.

The following verses from Psalm 107 parallel the experience of the Pilgrims and are a metaphoric picture of our own lives:

Some went down to the sea in ships.

. . .

. . . [God] commanded and raised the stormy wind,
  which lifted up the waves of the sea.

. . .

Then they cried to the LORD in their trouble.

. . .

  . . . He brought them to their desired haven.
Let them thank the LORD for his steadfast love,
  for his wondrous works to the children of man!
    (vv. 23, 25, 28, 30–31)

30

Evening Prayer

JANE AUSTEN

Father of Heaven! whose goodness has brought us in safety to the close of this day, dispose our hearts in fervent prayer. Another day is now gone, and added to those for which we were before accountable. Teach us Almighty Father, to consider this solemn truth, as we should do, that we may feel the importance of every day, and every hour as it passes, and earnestly strive to make a better use of what thy goodness may yet bestow on us, than we have done of the time past.

Give us grace to endeavor after a truly Christian spirit to seek to attain that temper of forbearance and patience of which our blessed Savior has set us the highest example; and which, while it prepares us for the spiritual happiness of the life to come, will secure to us the best enjoyment of what this world can give. Incline us, oh God! to think humbly of ourselves, to be severe only in the examination of our own conduct, to consider our fellow-creatures with kindness, and to judge of all they say and do with that charity which we would desire from them ourselves.

We thank thee with all our hearts for every gracious dispensation, for all the blessings that have attended our lives, for every hour of safety, health and peace, of domestic comfort and innocent enjoyment. We feel that we have been blessed far beyond anything that we have deserved; and though we cannot but pray for a continuance of all these mercies, we acknowledge our unworthiness of them and implore thee to pardon the presumption of our desires.

Keep us oh! Heavenly Father, from evil this night. Bring us in safety to the beginning of another day and grant that we may rise again with every serious and religious feeling which now directs us.

May thy mercy be extended over all mankind, bringing the ignorant to the knowledge of thy truth, awakening the impenitent, touching the hardened. Look with compassion upon the afflicted of every condition, assuage the pangs of disease, comfort the broken in spirit.

More particularly do we pray for the safety and welfare of our own family and friends wheresoever dispersed, beseeching thee to avert from them all material and lasting evil of body or mind; and may we by the assistance of thy Holy Spirit so conduct ourselves on earth as to secure an eternity of happiness with each other in thy heavenly kingdom. Grant this most merciful Father, for the sake of our blessed Savior in whose holy name and words we further address thee.

Our Father which are in heaven,
Hallowed be thy name.
Thy kingdom come,
Thy will be done,
in earth, as it is in heaven.
Give us this day our daily bread.
And forgive us our debts, as we forgive our debtors.
And lead us not into temptation, but deliver us from evil:
For thine is the kingdom, and the power, and the glory, forever.
Amen.[1]

Jane Austen (1775–1817) is one of the most famous British novelists of all time, with *Pride and Prejudice* being her best-known book. The father of her close-knit family was an Anglican minister, and the household routine included regular and lengthy evening devotions.

Three evening prayers composed by Jane Austen have survived, saved for posterity by her sister Cassandra. A prayer becomes a devotional when we allow it to direct our thoughts and feelings Godward and to meditate on the truths of the spiritual life.

The first key that unlocks Austen's beautiful composition is to read it as expressing spiritual sentiments that are appropriate at the end of a day. Whereas a morning prayer or meditation is *prospective*, looking forward to the day that will follow, an evening prayer or devotional is *retrospective*, casting a gaze backward on the day, in an awareness of the coming night as well. Looking for these end-of-day elements in Austen's prayer provides good analytic insights.

A second key to appreciating Austen's prayer is to notice how all-inclusive and comprehensive it is. Although it is only thirteen sentences long (not counting the Lord's Prayer at the end), it incorporates all of the standard elements of prayer—thanksgiving, confession, petition, and intercession for the needs of others—all permeated with an exaltation of God in a spirit of reverence and praise.

The stately style and verbal beauty are part of the devotional effect of Austen's prayer. These qualities flowed into Austen's artistic being from the King James Bible and Anglican Prayer Book, with which she had daily contact. The sentences are long, but they flow smoothly and are immediately understandable. The words too elevate our spirits because they rise above everyday colloquial discourse. The effect is elegance and reverence combined with simplicity.

It is a regular feature of liturgical traditions like the Anglican to end a prayer or meditation with the Lord's Prayer, which possesses the same balanced clauses and dignified language that Austen's prayer displays. Additionally, the Lord's Prayer can be assimilated as a devotional composition as well as a prayer if we pause on the individual elements and meditate on them.

Jane Austen's evening prayer has a calming effect, setting our spirits at rest in a twilight mood. Psalm 4:8 is cut from the same cloth:

> *In peace I will both lie down and sleep;*
> *for you alone, O L*ORD*, make me dwell in safety.*

31

What the Bible Means
to a Believer

THE GENEVA BIBLE AND KING JAMES VERSION

The word of God . . . is the light to our paths, the key of the
kingdom of heaven, our comfort in affliction, our shield and
sword against Satan, the school of all wisdom, the glass [win-
dow] wherein we behold God's face, the testimony of his favor,
and the . . . food and nourishment of our souls. Therefore, as
brethren that are partakers of the same hope and salvation with
us, we beseech you [our readers] that this rich pearl and inestimable treasure may not be offered in vain, but as sent from
God to the people of God, for the increase of his kingdom [and]
the comfort of his church, . . . so you might willingly receive the
word of God, earnestly study it and in all your life practice it,
that you may now appear in deed to be the people of God, . . .
that God in us may be fully glorified through Christ Jesus our
Lord, who liveth and reigneth forever. Amen.

From the Preface to the Geneva Bible
1560

It is not only an armor, but also a whole armory of weapons,
both offensive and defensive, whereby we may save ourselves
and put the enemy to flight. It is not an herb, but a tree, or

rather a whole paradise of trees of life, which bring forth fruit every month, and the fruit thereof is for food, and the leaves for medicine. It is not a pot of Manna, or a cruse of oil . . . , or for a meal's meat or two, but as it were a shower of heavenly bread sufficient for a whole host, be it never so great; and as it were a whole cellar full of oil vessels, whereby all our necessities may be provided for; and . . . finally a fountain of most pure water springing up unto everlasting life.

And what marvel [i.e., why should that seem surprising]? The original thereof being from heaven, not from earth; the author being God, not man . . . ; the matter [content], verity [truth], piety, purity, uprightness; the form, God's word, God's testimony, God's oracles, the word of truth, the word of salvation; the effects, light of understanding, stableness of persuasion, repentance from dead works, newness of life, holiness, peace, joy in the Holy Ghost; lastly, the end and reward of the study thereof, fellowship with the Saints, participation of the heavenly nature, fruition of an inheritance immortal, undefiled, and that never shall fade away. Happy is the one that delighteth in the Scripture, and thrice happy that meditates in it day and night.[1]

From "The Translators to the Reader," King James Version
1611

———— ⊗⊗⊗ ————

The prefaces to English Bible translations are an untapped treasury of devotional riches. Naturally these prefaces devote the most space to laying out the technicalities of translation and the translation philosophy of the committee. But because the scholars' work on the translation is the most important work of their lives, they also want to declare the spiritual purpose of their book and the hoped-for effect in their readers' lives.

The splendor of the two passages printed here exists at a macro level and a micro level. At the global level, we are swept up by the stylistic majesty of the passages. This is known as the high style, designed to fulfill the principle that high thoughts must have high language. The main content of the passages is expressed in only five long sentences.

The rhetorical technique consists of stringing together a succession of parallel phrases and clauses that draw us into a great onward march. And in a further marvel, so much is packed into these five sentences that they are nothing less than a complete primer on the nature and effects of the Bible.

At the micro level, every phrase and image and metaphor beckons us to linger lovingly on it. When we do this, the first thing we note is the general quality of verbal beauty. Then we need to remember that images, metaphors, and epithets (titles) need to have their meanings unpacked, as we determine (for example) *how* the Bible is a *light* or *food* or a *fountain*. Not all images are visual or sensory; conceptual images name qualities rather than things. In the passages here, therefore, we need to explore the meanings of the great abstractions that figure prominently—conceptual images such as *purity* and *uprightness* and *holiness*.

The two prefaces perform for us the goals of any good devotional. They awaken our religious affections, codify our understanding of the truth, remind us of the spiritual riches that we possess, confirm us in the Christian faith, and express what we wish to affirm, but in words more beautiful and powerful than we ourselves can produce.

The Bible's self-testimony to its own nature is a leading biblical theme, and the passages printed here are a good summary of these scriptural claims. Among the Bible's memorable claims about itself is 2 Timothy 3:16–17: "All Scripture is breathed out by God and profitable for teaching, for reproof, for correction, and for training in righteousness, that the man of God may be complete, equipped for every good work."

32

The Almost Christian

JOHN WESLEY

Ever since the Christian religion was in the world, there have been many in every age and nation who were almost persuaded to be Christians. But seeing it avails nothing before God to go only thus far, it highly imports us to consider . . . [what] is implied in being altogether a Christian. I answer:

First. The love of God. . . . Such a love is this, as engrosses the whole heart, as rakes up all the affections, as fills the entire capacity of the soul and employs the utmost extent of all its faculties. He that thus loves the Lord his God, his spirit continually "rejoiceth in God his Savior." His delight is in the Lord. . . . All his desire is unto God, and to the remembrance of his name. . . .

The second thing implied in the being altogether a Christian is the love of our neighbor. . . . If any man ask, "Who is my neighbor," we reply, Every man in the world; every child of his who is the Father of the spirits of all flesh. Nor may we in any wise except our enemies or the enemies of God and their own souls. But every Christian loveth these also as himself. . . .

There is yet one thing more that may be separately considered, though it cannot actually be separate from the preceding, which is implied in the being altogether a Christian; and that is the ground of all, even faith. . . . The right and true Christian faith is . . . not only to believe that Holy Scripture and the Articles of our Faith are true, but also to have a sure trust and confidence to be saved from everlasting damnation by Christ. It is a sure trust and confidence which a man hath in God, that, by the merits of Christ, his sins are forgiven, and he reconciled to the favor of God; whereof doth follow a loving heart, to obey his commandments. . . .

Do good designs and good desires make a Christian? By no means, unless they are brought to good effect. "Hell is paved," saith one, "with good intentions." The great question of all, then, still remains. Is the love of God shed abroad in your heart? . . . Do you desire nothing but him? Are you happy in God? Is he your glory, your delight, your crown of rejoicing? . . . Do you love your neighbor as yourself? . . . Hast thou indeed redemption through [Christ's] blood, even the remission of thy sins? And doth his Spirit bear witness with thy spirit, that thou art a child of God? . . .

May we all thus experience what it is to be, not almost only, but altogether Christians; being justified freely by his grace, through the redemption that is in Jesus; knowing we have peace with God through Jesus Christ; rejoicing in hope of the glory of God; and having the love of God shed abroad in our hearts, by the Holy Spirit given unto us![1]

John Wesley (1703–1791) did not coin the evocative label "almost Christian." The Puritan Matthew Mead had published a treatise titled *The Almost Christian Discovered* in 1661, and Wesley's fellow evangelist George Whitfield preached a sermon titled "The Almost Christian" two years before Wesley preached this sermon at Oxford University on July 25, 1741. In some circles this sermon is considered to be Wesley's most famous sermon.[2]

In the first half of the sermon, Wesley develops a list of ways in which a person can exhibit many of the traits of being a Christian while still falling short of true belief leading to eternal life. According to Wesley and his forerunners on this theme, people can live a life of Christian morality, can attend church and pray, and can assent to

Christian doctrine without being a true Christian. In a poignant moment in the middle of the sermon, Wesley confides that for many years he was in the category of almost Christian, earnestly desiring to serve God but not being a genuine Christian. Having made this confession, Wesley turns in the second half of the sermon to the question, "What more than this *is implied in the being altogether a Christian?*"

Wesley answers his question in a partly unexpected way. We know beforehand that he will say that a true believer trusts in Jesus as Savior from sin, but few of us would choose the twofold summary of the law—loving God above all and our neighbor as ourselves—as the template on which we would build our definition. Similarly, in regard to loving our neighbor, we are caught off guard by how insistent Wesley is that we must love our enemies as ourselves.

Several avenues exist to application. Wesley offers his sermon as a safety check on our own spiritual state. We can then extend that to our concern for the souls of family and friends. Additionally, as Wesley fills out his criteria for being a true Christian, he raises the bar very high in regard to loving God and our neighbor, thereby inviting us to strive for a higher level of attainment than we currently possess. While seeming only to *define* what it means to be a Christian, under the surface Wesley's rhetorical or persuasive strategy is to shake us out of whatever lethargy exists in our own Christian walks. Even if we are true Christians, there is something in Wesley's words to prompt a holy discontent with our current spiritual state.

The text on which Wesley bases his diagnosis of how to know if we are a true Christian is the following dramatic moment after the apostle Paul had recounted the story of his conversion to King Agrippa: "'King Agrippa, believest thou the prophets? I know that thou believest.' Then Agrippa said unto Paul, 'Almost thou persuadest me to be a Christian'" (Acts 26:27–28 KJV).

33

The Estate of Marriage

MARTIN LUTHER

The estate of marriage is something quite different from merely being married. He who is married but does not recognize the estate of marriage cannot continue in wedlock without bitterness, drudgery, and anguish. . . . But he who recognizes the estate of marriage will find therein delight, love, and joy without end. . . .

Now the ones who recognize the estate of marriage are those who firmly believe that God himself instituted it, brought husband and wife together, and ordained that they should beget children and care for them. For this they have God's word (Gen. 1:28), and they can be certain that he does not lie. They can therefore also be certain that the estate of marriage and everything that goes with it in the way of conduct, works, and suffering is pleasing to God. Now tell me, how can the heart have greater good, joy, and delight than in God, when one is certain that his estate, conduct, and work is pleasing to God?

Now observe that when . . . our natural reason . . . takes a look at married life, she turns up her nose and says, "Alas, must I rock the baby, wash its diapers, make its bed, smell its stench, stay up nights with it, take care of it when it cries, heal its rashes and sores, and on top of that care for my wife, provide for her, labor at my trade, take care of this and take care of that, do this and do that, endure this and endure that, and whatever else of bitterness and drudgery married life involves? What, should I make such a prisoner of myself? . . ."

What then does Christian faith say to this? It opens its eyes, looks upon all these insignificant, distasteful, and despised duties in the Spirit, and is aware that they are all adorned with divine approval as with the costliest gold and jewels. It says, "O God, because I am certain that thou hast created me as a man and hast from my body begotten this child, I also know for a certainty that it meets with thy perfect pleasure. I confess to thee that I am not worthy to rock the little babe or wash its diapers, or to be entrusted with the care of the child and its mother. How is it that I, without any merit, have come to this distinction of being certain that I am serving thy creature and thy most precious will? O how gladly will I do so, though the duties should be even more insignificant and despised. . . ."

A wife too should regard her duties in the same light, as she suckles the child, rocks and bathes it, and cares for it in other ways; and as she busies herself with other duties and renders help and obedience to her husband. These are truly golden and noble works. . . . When a father goes ahead and washes diapers or performs some other mean task for his child . . . , God, with all his angels and creatures, is smiling, not because that father is washing diapers, but because he is doing so in Christian faith.[1]

The context within which we must understand this famous passage is the transformation that the Reformation effected in regard to the doctrine of calling or vocation, and the resultant elevation of common work and duties in people's valuation. No Reformer contributed more to this revolution of thinking than Martin Luther (1483–1546). A sometimes overlooked nuance is that the idea of calling extended not only to one's chief occupation in life but also to all of the roles and duties that God places before us. For Luther, "the life of the home, the relation between parents and children, is vocation."[2]

Within this framework, everything in the passage falls into place. We should note first that throughout the passage Luther does not regard domestic duties as self-contained activities but rather as activities carried out in obedience to what God demands of parents. This doctrinal framework is set forth in the two opening paragraphs, where Luther elevates marriage to an estate instituted by God.

But of course the unbelieving mind does acknowledge this distinction. Luther attributes this secular mindset to our faculty of reason, which is set over against the Christian faith. A great contrast thus underlies the passage, and Luther arranges the passage as a story that records a momentous attitude adjustment.

The passage gains its vigor through Luther's creative imagination. It is the impulse of the imagination to show rather than tell—to embody rather than state something abstractly. First, then, Luther personifies both human reason and Christian faith, giving each a vigorous speaking part. Then Luther's realistic imagination takes over, as he pictures the details of everyday domestic duties in regard in care of an infant, with emphasis on the smelly details of changing a diaper. Finally, God's approval is not a mere abstraction but is pictured as a crowd of onlookers and a cosmic cheering section.

The main idea of Luther's passage is that common work is a calling from God and something to be performed as an act of obedience to God. Colossians 3:23–24 sounds the same note: "Whatever you do, work heartily, as for the Lord and not for men, knowing that from the Lord you will receive the inheritance as your reward. You are serving the Lord Christ."

34

Death as a Welcome Sleep

John Donne

To those that die in Christ, death is but a sleep; to all others, death is . . . literally death. . . . The death of the righteous is a sleep; first, as it delivers them to a present rest. Now men sleep not well fasting; nor does a fasting conscience, a conscience that is not nourished with a testimony of having done well, come to this sleep. . . . To him that laboreth in his calling, even this sleep of death is welcome. When thou liest down thou shalt not be afraid, saith Solomon [Prov. 3:24]. . . .

So then this death is a sleep, as it delivers us to a present rest; and then, lastly, it is so also as it promises a future . . . glorious resurrection. To the wicked it is far from both: of them God says [that] they shall sleep a perpetual sleep and not awake; they shall have no part in the second resurrection. But for them that have slept in Christ, as Christ said of Lazarus, "Lazarus sleepeth, but I go that I may wake him out of sleep," he shall say to his Father, Let me go that I may wake them who have slept so long in expectation of my coming: and those that sleep in Jesus Christ (saith the apostle) [1 Thess. 4:15–17] will God bring with him; not only fetch them out of the dust when he comes, but bring them with him, that is, declare that they have been in his hands ever since they departed out of this world.

They shall awake as Jacob did, and say as Jacob said, Surely the Lord is in this place, and this is no other but the house of

God, and the gate of heaven, and into that gate they shall enter, and in that house they shall dwell, where there shall be no cloud nor sun, no darkness nor dazzling, but one equal light, no noise nor silence, but one equal music, no fears nor hopes, but one equal possession, no foes nor friends, but an equal communion and identity, no ends nor beginnings, but one equal eternity. Keep us Lord so awake in the duties of our callings, that we may thus sleep in thy peace, and wake in thy glory, and change that infallibility which thou affordest us here, to an actual and undeterminable possession of that kingdom which thy Son our Savior Christ Jesus hath purchased for us, with the inestimable price of his incorruptible blood. Amen.[1]

John Donne (1572–1631) is one of the most famous preachers in English church history, but his sermons do not resemble the ones with which we are familiar. They follow the stream of Donne's thinking and follow many byways under a main topic or Bible verse. Allusions to the Bible and other texts abound. Additionally, Donne excelled at paradox and metaphor. While these traits make his sermons nearly impossible to assimilate as sermons that we might hear as we sit in a church pew, they lend themselves to contemplation as packed devotional passages.

Donne's subject in the passage printed here is the death of the righteous. But at once complexity and paradox enter the picture. Donne gets us to see that the death of the righteous is both a sleep and a waking. As part of Donne's love of complexity, in the middle paragraph he brings in the nuance that those who have been asleep in physical death have at the same time been alive in God's presence (an inference from 1 Thess. 4:15–17).

The crown jewel of this passage is the long sentence at the start of the final paragraph that employs the rhetorical pattern of *no . . . nor . . . but*, with the added ingredient of antithesis (joining of opposites). Before we unpack the meanings of this famous sentence, we should note some external facts about it. Although Donne *declares* that believers *shall enter* the gate of God's house, the most common form in which the passage lives on in our culture is a petitionary prayer that begins, "*Bring us,* O Lord God. . . ." This passage is extremely well known, with an internet search yielding several dozen sites that quote the passage. Additionally, the words have been set to music by several composers and is a familiar offering in liturgical choral circles, especially in England.

What accounts for the power of this famous sentence? The passage awakens our awareness of the contradictions of life in a fallen world—light and darkness, noise and silence, foes and friends. Then it taps into our longing for repose—for a peaceable and predictable existence that transcends the flux and inconstancy in our lives. Rhetorically, the passage consists of a series of parallel phrases, each one consisting of paired opposites.

If we broaden our gaze to the passage as a whole, we can see that a grand paradox underlies it. Death is declared to be both a sleep (the first two paragraphs) and a waking (final paragraph). And then a further paradox emerges when the *waking* at the final resurrection is portrayed as having the qualities of eternal *rest* as the sleep of death has earlier been said to possess.

Donne's entire sermon, which roams over much in addition to the concluding meditation on death and heaven, takes its origin from a simple statement in the account of Stephen's martyrdom in Acts 7: "And when he had said this, he fell asleep" (v. 60).

35

Morning and Evening

Charles Spurgeon

Morning, July 9

"Forget not all His benefits."

Psalm 103:2

It is a delightful and profitable occupation to mark the hand of God in the lives of ancient saints, and to observe his goodness in delivering them, his mercy in pardoning them, and his faithfulness in keeping his covenant with them. But would it not be even more interesting and profitable for us to remark the hand of God in our own lives? Ought we not to look upon our own history as being at least as full of God, as full of his goodness and of his truth, as much a proof of his faithfulness and veracity, as the lives of any of the saints who have gone before? We do our Lord an injustice when we suppose that he wrought all his mighty acts, and showed himself strong for those in the early time, but doth not perform wonders or lay bare his arm for the saints who are now upon the earth.

Let us review our own lives. Surely in these we may discover some happy incidents, refreshing to ourselves and glorifying to our God. Have you had no deliverances? Have you passed through no rivers, supported by the divine presence? Have you walked through no fires unharmed? Have you had no manifestations? Have you had no choice favors? . . . Have you never been made to lie down in green pastures? Have you never been led by the still waters? Surely the goodness of God has been the same to us as to the saints of old. Let us, then, weave his mercies into a song. Let us take the pure gold of thankfulness, and the jewels of praise and make them into another crown for the head of Jesus.

Evening, July 9

> *"And God divided the light from the darkness."*
> GENESIS 1:4

A believer has two principles at work within him. In his natural estate he was subject to one principle only, which was darkness; now light has entered, and the two principles disagree. . . . How is this state of things occasioned? "The Lord divided the light from the darkness." Darkness, by itself, is quiet and undisturbed, but when the Lord sends in light, there is a conflict, for the one is in opposition to the other: a conflict which will never cease till the believer is altogether light in the Lord.

If there be a division within the individual Christian, there is certain to be a division without. So soon as the Lord gives to any man light, he proceeds to separate himself from the darkness around; he secedes from a merely worldly religion of outward ceremonial, for nothing short of the gospel of Christ will now satisfy him, and he withdraws himself from worldly society and frivolous amusements, and seeks the company of the saints. . . . The light gathers to itself, and the darkness to itself. What God has divided, let us never try to unite. . . . We are to be nonconformists to the world, dissenting from all sin, and distinguished from the rest of mankind by our likeness to our Master.[1]

Today there are over four hundred daily devotional guides for sale. What is the origin of this flourishing enterprise? There can be little doubt that it started in 1866 with Charles Spurgeon (1834–1892), who remains the giant in the landscape.

In his autobiography, Spurgeon himself lets us in on the genesis of his book. He decided to experiment with a years' worth of morning devotionals, published under the title *Morning by Morning*. Within two years, a sequel appeared as *Evening by Evening*, and later these were combined to form the familiar classic. Spurgeon began with the conviction that "the vice of many religious works is their dullness" and predictability. So he consciously cultivated variety and freshness, "changing our method constantly." The genres included exhortation, personal meditation, and conversation. Having decided to slant each devotional around a Bible verse, Spurgeon "selected unusual texts" and took up "neglected topics."[2]

All of this was a formula for success. Today Spurgeon's *Morning and Evening* is available in over one hundred print and electronic forms.

The excerpted entries for July 9 are typical of the book as a whole. Each one puts a Bible verse before us to focus our attention. But the devotional is not an exposition of the verse, which is instead a launching pad for the meditation that follows. Psalm 103:2, part of the psalmist's exhortation to his soul not to forget God's benefits, leads Spurgeon to exhort his readers to recall God's providential favors in their lives. The passage is filled with rhetorical questions that prompt readers to assent to the claims that God has acted on their behalf. It is a call to action.

The evening meditation quotes from the Bible's creation account, but it is not about God's creation of the world. Spurgeon turns the statement that God divided the light from the darkness into a metaphor of the spiritual life. In Spurgeon's imaginative handling, dividing the light from the darkness becomes a principle of Christian living—a call to shun evil and walk in the light of God. Both passages show that Spurgeon has the gifts of a poet, as his devotional writing soars on the wings of the imagination.

Part of the genius of Spurgeon's famous book is its title. The reason the title strikes such a familiar note is that daily worship in Old Testament times tied into the rhythm of morning and evening. Psalm 92:1–2 is a passage that fixes this in our memory:

> *It is good to give thanks to the LORD,*
>   *to sing praises to your name, O Most High;*
> *to declare your steadfast love in the morning,*
>   *and your faithfulness by night.*

36

The Mystery of Providence

JOHN FLAVEL

It is the duty of the saints . . . to reflect upon the performances of Providence for them in all the states and through all the stages of their lives. . . .

The respect and relation Providence bears to our prayers is of singular consideration, and a most taking and sweet meditation. Prayer honors Providence, and Providence honors prayer. . . .

[By meditating on God's providence] you may maintain sweet and conscious communion with God from day to day. And what is more desirable in this world in comparison with that . . . ? A great part of the pleasure and delight of the Christian life is made out of the observations of Providence. . . .

There are leading providences which, however slight and trivial they may seem in themselves, yet . . . they usher in a multitude of other mercies, and draw a blessed train of happy consequence after them. . . . Have we not with joy observed how those very things that sense and reason tell us are opposite to our happiness have been the most blessed instruments to promote it! . . . [God] shows Himself to spiritual eyes in the providences, as clearly as the sun manifests itself by its own beams of light. . . .

The goodness and mercy of God to His people is seen in His providence concerning them; and this is the very root of praise. It is not so much the possession that Providence gives us of such or such comforts as the goodness and kindness of God in the dispensing of them that engages a gracious soul to praise. . . . To give, maintain, and preserve our life are choice acts of Providence, but to do all this in a way of grace and lovingkindness, this is far better than the gifts themselves. Life is but the shadow of death without it. This is the mercy that crowns all other mercies. . . .

Let us . . . consider how the several changes and removes of our lives have been ordered for us. Things we never foresaw have been all along ordered for us. The way of man is not in himself. God's thoughts have not been our thoughts, nor His ways our ways. Among the eminent mercies of your life, reader, how many of them have been mere surprises to you! Your own projects have been thrust aside to make way for better things designed by Providence for you. . . .

At death the people of God receive the last mercies that they shall ever receive in this world by the hand of Providence, and are immediately to make up their accounts with God for all the mercies that ever they received from His hand. What can be more suitable therefore to a dying person than to recount with himself the mercies of his whole life, and manifold receipts of favor for which he is to reckon with God speedily. And how shall this be done without a due and serious observation and recording of them now? . . .

Indeed, it were not worthwhile to live in a world devoid of God and Providence.[1]

Next to the way of salvation in Christ, the doctrine that unleashed the greatest wellsprings of Puritan spiritual sentiment was providence. Puritan poet John Milton said in the purpose statement of his epic *Paradise Lost* that he intended to "assert eternal providence," and at the very end of the story, as Adam and Eve are expelled from the garden, their climactic consolation is encapsulated in the phrase "and providence their guide."[2]

John Flavel (1628–1691) was a Puritan preacher and author of some thirty books. His book on providence is a complete treatment of the topic, touching upon such aspects of providence as its nature, the spheres in which it operates (childhood, conversion, family life, etc.), the need for believers to meditate on God's acts of providence in their lives, and the practical uses to which we can put such contemplation. In view of this comprehensiveness, it would have been accurate to title the book the *consolations* of providence, but Flavel chose to accentuate the *mystery* of it.

The passages brought together to form the selection in this anthology are unified by this theme of mystery. Each of the brief paragraphs uncovers for us a surprising or unexpected or unnoticed dimension of providence. Examples are the way in which externally minor or seemingly negative events in our lives are actually momentous and positive in their effects, the way in which we could never have arranged the train of events in our life by human means, the connection between prayer and events of providence, and the suggestion that the greatest use of remembering God's acts of providence will come in the hours leading up to our death.

The greatest achievement of Flavel's meditation on the mystery of providence is that he presents providence not only as a doctrine but also as a reality that can become a source of daily spiritual strength to us and a means of relating personally to God. But this will happen only if we follow Flavel's prompts for meditating on God's acts of providence in our lives.

—⊗⊗⊗—

The main thrust of Flavel's treatise on providence is that we need to observe God's providence in our lives, to rehearse God's providential acts to ourselves, and to praise God for them. This is exactly what the writer of Psalm 103 does, starting with the first two verses:

> *Bless the* Lord, *O my soul,*
> *and all that is within me,*
> *bless his holy name!*
> *Bless the* Lord, *O my soul,*
> *and forget not all his benefits. (vv. 1–2)*

37

The Believer's New Name

GEORGE MACDONALD

*To him that overcometh, I will give a white stone,
and in the stone a new name written, which no
man knoweth saving he that receiveth it.*

REVELATION 2:17

Not only then has each one an *individual* relation to God, but each has a *peculiar* [unique] relation to God. He is to God a peculiar being, made after his own fashion, and that of no one else; for when he is perfected he shall receive the new name which no one else can understand. Hence he can worship God as no one else can worship him, can understand God as no one else can understand him. This or that one may understand God more, may understand God better than he, but no other one can understand God as he understands him. . . . As the fir tree lifts up itself with a far different need from the need of the palm tree, so does each one stand before God, and lift up a different humanity to the common Father. And for each, God has a different response. With every one he has a secret—the secret of the new name. In every one there is a loneliness, an inner chamber of peculiar life into which God only can enter. . . .

From this it follows that there is a chamber also . . . in God himself into which none can enter but the one, the individual, the peculiar one, out of which chamber that one has to bring revelation and strength for his brethren. This is that for which he was made—to reveal the secret things of the Father. By his creation, then, each one is isolated with God; each, in respect of his peculiar making, can say, "*my* God"; each can come to him alone, and speak with him face to face, as a man speaks with his friend. . . .

See, now, what a significance the symbolism of our text assumes. Each of us is a distinct flower or tree in the spiritual garden of God, precious, each for his own sake, in the eyes of him who is even now making us, each of us watered and shone upon and filled with life, for the sake of his flower, his completed being, which will blossom out of him at last to the glory and pleasure of the great gardener. For each has within him a secret of the Divinity; each is growing towards the revelation of that secret to himself, and so to the full reception, according to his measure, of the divine. Every moment that he is true to his true self, some new shine of the white stone breaks on his inward eye, some fresh channel is opened upward for the coming glory of the flower, the conscious offering of his whole being in beauty to the Maker.

Each one, then, is in God's sight worthy. Life and action, thought and intent, are sacred. And what an end lies before us! To have a consciousness of our own ideal being flashed into us from the thought of God![1]

George MacDonald (1824–1905) was a Victorian Scottish minister and literary author. His ministerial life was eclipsed by his literary life, especially his pioneering works of fantasy writing. His influence on literary Christian fantasy writers is as noteworthy as his own literary production. C. S. Lewis regarded MacDonald as his "master," paying tribute to him by publishing an entire anthology of quotations from him. Regarding *Unspoken Sermons* (from which the selection here is taken), Lewis claimed that "my own debt to this book is almost as great as one man can owe to another."[2]

The intriguing idea of unspoken sermons has a biographical explanation. When MacDonald resigned from a pastoral life with preaching responsibilities, the sermons he composed were not intended for delivery from a pulpit. His unspoken sermons have a quality akin to what we expect in devotional writing, as seen in the passage printed here.

MacDonald's original twist of mind emerges at once by virtue of the text that he chose as a springboard for meditation. Revelation 2:17 is so baffling that our tendency is to read right past it. MacDonald compels us to ponder its mystery as he teases out the meanings of a symbolic *white stone* bearing a name known only to God and us individually. Without this rootedness in the Bible, MacDonald's bold claims for our individual identity in Christ would seem excessive. The takeaway for us is double: (1) it generates our gratitude to God for the intimacy of his dealings with us personally, and (2) it prompts us to take our spiritual responsibilities more seriously, knowing that we are so individually known to God.

Isaiah 43:1 is an Old Testament parallel to Revelation 2:17 on how God knows his followers by name:

> *Fear not, for I have redeemed you;*
> *I have called you by name, you are mine.*

38

Reflections on Mortality and Immortality

PRAYER BOOK'S BURIAL SERVICE

Man that is born of a woman hath but a short time to live, and is full of misery. He cometh up, and is cut down, like a flower; he fleeth as it were a shadow, and never continueth in one stay. In the midst of life we are in death: of whom may we seek for help, but of thee, O Lord, who for our sins art justly displeased? Yet, O Lord God most holy, O Lord most mighty, O holy and most merciful Savior, deliver us not into the bitter pains of eternal death . . . [and] suffer us not, at our last hour, for any pains of death, to fall from thee.

Forasmuch as it hath pleased Almighty God, in his wise providence, to take out of this world the soul of our deceased brother/sister, we therefore commit the body to the ground; earth to earth, ashes to ashes, dust to dust; looking for the general Resurrection in the last day, and the life of the world to come, through our Lord Jesus Christ; at whose second coming in glorious majesty to judge the world, the earth and the sea shall give up their dead; and the corruptible bodies of those who sleep in him shall be changed, and made like unto his own glorious body; according to the mighty working whereby he is able to subdue all things unto himself. . . .

Almighty God, with whom do live the spirits of those who depart hence in the Lord, and with whom the souls of the faithful, after they are delivered from the burden of the flesh, are in joy and felicity: we give thee hearty thanks for the good examples of all those thy servants, who, having finished their course in faith, do now rest from their labors. And we beseech thee, that we, with all those who are departed in the true faith of thy holy Name, may have our perfect consummation and bliss, both in body and soul, in thy eternal and everlasting glory; through Jesus Christ our Lord. Amen.

O merciful God, the Father of our Lord Jesus Christ, who is the resurrection and the life; in whom whosoever believeth, shall live, though he die; and whosoever liveth, and believeth in him, shall not die eternally; who also hath taught us, by his holy Apostle Saint Paul, not to be sorry, as men without hope, for those who sleep in him.

We humbly beseech thee, O Father, to raise us from the death of sin unto the life of righteousness; that, when we shall depart this life, we may rest in him; and that, at the general Resurrection in the last day, we may be found acceptable in thy sight; and receive that blessing, which thy well-beloved Son shall then pronounce to all who love and fear thee, saying, Come, ye blessed children of my Father, receive the kingdom prepared for you from the beginning of the world.[1]

This passage is obviously phrased in the highest of the high style. The language is stately and exalted. The sentences are long. Parallelism of phrases and clauses abounds, as do lofty epithets (titles) for God, such as *Lord God most holy*. All of this is appropriate, inasmuch as solemn events such as death call for formality and dignity. The very beauty of this moving meditation of mortality and immortality is itself consoling, which is what a burial service needs to be. Additionally, all that affirms order in a time of crisis is consoling, and the mastery of verbal beauty and sentence structure such as we find in the burial service is a form of order.

The passage moves back and forth like a pendulum between the two poles of realistic acknowledgment of human mortality on the one hand and faith in all that the Bible teaches about immortality on the other. We welcome both of these.

We certainly do not want a denial of human mutability and the facts of death as we contemplate a coffin and the corpse within it. So right from the start the burial service wins us with its realistic imagery of death, of burial, of human misery and sinfulness, of eternal death for those who die without belief in Jesus.

But we long even more for the certainties of the Christian faith regarding immortality, resurrection from death, and eternal life with God in heaven. So the burial service speaks rapturously and at even greater length about these realities. Part of what makes the burial service great is the deliberate juxtaposition of death and life. All the way through, we move from one to the other, often in the same sentence.

All that has been said thus far commends the burial service for its intended purpose as a public event. What about the suggested purpose of a personal devotional? We should absorb the passage as a dress rehearsal for our own death, burial, and entry into life everlasting.

⸺⸺∽∾⸺⸺

The burial service is so permeated by biblical phraseology and allusions that it may seem a little arbitrary to single out the following passage, but it is certainly one of the Bible's greatest passages on the subject of this devotional: "Jesus said to [Martha], 'I am the resurrection and the life. Whoever believes in me, though he die, yet shall he live, and everyone who lives and believes in me shall never die. Do you believe this?'" (John 11:25–26).

39

The World as the Theater of God's Glory

John Calvin

The world . . . is a theater erected for displaying the glory of God. . . . Let us not disdain to receive a pious delight from the works of God, which everywhere present themselves to view in this very beautiful theater of the world. . . . Everyone should seriously apply himself to a consideration of the works of God, being placed in this very splendid theater to be a spectator of them. . . .

If we consider for what end [God] has created the various kinds of food, we shall find that he intended to provide not only for our necessity, but likewise for our pleasure and delight. So in clothing, he has had in view not mere necessity, but propriety and decency. In herbs, trees, and fruits, beside their various uses, his design has been to gratify us by graceful forms and pleasant odors. . . . And even the natural properties of things sufficiently indicate for what end, and to what extent, it is lawful to use them. But shall the Lord have endued flowers with such beauty, to present itself to our eyes, with such sweetness of smell, to impress our sense of smelling; and shall it be unlawful for our eyes to be affected with the beautiful sight, or our olfactory nerves with the agreeable odor? What! has he not made such a distinction of colors as to render some more agreeable than others? Has he not given to gold and silver, to ivory and marble, a beauty which makes them more precious than other metals or stones? In a word, has he not made many things worthy of our estimation, independently of any necessary use? . . .

For this . . . is, in the order of nature, the first lesson of faith, to remember that, whithersoever we turn our eyes, all the things which we behold are the works of God; and at the same time to consider, with pious meditation, for what end God created them. . . . [God] has wonderfully adorned heaven and earth with the utmost possible abundance, variety, and beauty, like a large and splendid mansion, most exquisitely and copiously furnished. . . . It is undoubtedly the will of the Lord, that we should be continually employed in this holy meditation; that, while we contemplate in all the creatures, as in so many mirrors, the infinite riches of his wisdom, justice, goodness, and power, we might not only take a transient and cursory view of them, but might long dwell on the idea, seriously and faithfully revolve it in our minds, and frequently recall it to our memory.[1]

The subject of this devotional is what the Puritans called "the goods" and "the creatures" of this world. By this they meant the earthly gifts that God bestows on the entire human race. These gifts fall into the categories of the natural creation and human culture. In his masterwork *Institutes of the Christian Religion*, John Calvin (1509–1564) sounds an important keynote of the Reformation when he asserts repeatedly that God intends us to enjoy the "goods" of life in moderation and with gratitude to God as their giver.

Calvin formulated a famous metaphor by which to denote the composite gifts of nature and culture. It is that the world is the theater of God's glory. The first paragraph of the devotional printed here consists of three sentences from separate places in the *Institutes* where Calvin sets forth this metaphor. As we unpack the metaphor, we become aware of certain things about God's creation and us as inhabitants of it. God's glory is on display. We are spectators of it. It is in the nature of a theatrical performance that a dynamic interaction exists between the audience and the performers. The result of this interaction is pleasure and delight. And so forth.

With this theoretic framework in place, the rest of Calvin's meditation is a lyrical celebration of the delights of nature that are all around us for the taking. The structure of this celebration is an inventory of beautiful and pleasurable features of nature and human life. Calvin brings to our awareness the everyday splendors that our daily routine tends to obscure. The devotional takeaway is that we need to be attentive to God's gifts in creation and culture, and to render worship to him. Along with the celebration of the senses, there is an undertow of exhortation to the effect that God expects us to ascend in our contemplation from the earthly gifts to the divine giver.

—⚬⚬⚬—

Calvin and his heirs the Puritans presented a unified voice in affirming that God has given us the good things of life for our enjoyment, not for our rejection. First Timothy 6:17 became a key verse in the movement, with its command to "trust . . . in the living God, who giveth us richly all things to enjoy" (KJV).

40

Holiness

J. C. RYLE

A Woman to Be Remembered

The history of [the sin of Lot's wife] is given by the Holy Ghost in few and simple words—"She looked back from behind her husband, and she became a pillar of salt." We are told no more than this. There is a naked solemnity about the history. The sum and substance of her transgression lies in these three words, "She looked back." . . . Does the fault of Lot's wife appear a trifling one to be visited with such a punishment? There was far more in that look than strikes you at first sight: it implied far more than it expressed. . . .

That look was a little thing, but it revealed the true character of Lot's wife. Little things will often show the state of a person's mind even better than great ones, and little symptoms are often the signs of deadly and incurable diseases. . . . A little cough in a morning seems an unimportant ailment, but it is often an evidence of failing in the constitution. . . .

That look was a little thing, but *it told of secret love of the world* in Lot's wife. Her heart was in Sodom, though her body was outside. She had left her affections behind when she fled from her home. Her eye turned to the place where her treasure was, as the compass-needle turns to the pole. And this was the crowning point of her sin. . . . Lot's wife was lost by looking back to the world. . . . *The immense danger of worldliness* is the grand lesson which the Lord Jesus means us to learn. . . .

Beware of a half-hearted religion. . . . Let your religion be real. See that you do not sin the *sin of Lot's wife*. . . . I urge on every professing Christian who wishes to be happy the immense importance of making no compromise between God and the world. Do not . . . give Christ as little of your heart as possible, and keep as much as possible of the things of this life.

If you desire to be a healthy Christian, *consider often what your own end will be*. Will it be happiness, or will it be misery? Will it be the death of the righteous, or will it be a death without hope, like that of Lot's wife? You cannot live always: there must be an end one day. The last sermon will one day be heard; the last prayer will one day be prayed; the last chapter in the Bible will one day be read—meaning, wishing, hoping, intending, resolving, doubting, hesitating—all will at length be over. . . . There is mercy in God, like a river—but it is for the penitent believer in Christ Jesus. There is a love in God towards sinners which is unspeakable and unsearchable—but it is for those who "hear Christ's voice and follow Him." Seek to have an interest in that love. . . .

You have seen the history of Lot's wife—her privileges, her sin, and her end. You have been told of the uselessness of privileges without the gift of the Holy Ghost, of the danger of worldliness, and of the reality of hell. . . . I desire to set up a beacon to preserve souls from shipwreck. . . .[1]

The enthusiasm of devotees of J. C. Ryle (1816–1900), an evangelical Anglican bishop, is breathtaking. J. I. Packer said about Ryle's signature book *Holiness* (from which the devotional printed here was taken) that "Christians will find it a gold mine, a feast, a spur and a heart-warmer, food, drink, medicine, and a course of vitamins, all in one."[2] Such enthusiasm bears looking into.

Ryle quickly aligns himself with other entries in this anthology by springing surprises on us and overcoming the cliché effect of conventional platitudes about the Christian life. We assume that a book titled *Holiness* will be filled with positive directives and formulas that we can put into practice to achieve holiness. That assumption is immediately challenged by the book's subtitle—*Its Nature, Hindrances, Difficulties, and Roots*. When we see the sermon title "A Woman to Be Remembered," we assume that the sermon will be about a heroine like Ruth—a model to be emulated. Instead Ryle presents a negative example to be avoided. Ryle's approach to holiness is to explore the obstacles that get in its way and prevent its attainment.

This excerpted passage is typical of the book in this and other ways. Ryle's message is built around Jesus's cryptic command to "remember Lot's wife" (Luke 17:32). To explore how we can obey that command, Ryle takes us back to the equally terse story in which Lot's wife "looked back, and . . . became a pillar of salt" (Gen. 19:26). The genius of Ryle's meditation is his skill in unpacking the symbolism of this matter-of-fact narrative account. His methodology is what literary scholars call "close reading of a text," and then Ryle adds the preacher's instinct to exhort, admonish, and apply the words of Scripture to our lives. Samuel Taylor Coleridge claimed that the words of the Bible find us at the deepest level of our being; Ryle's analysis of "A Woman to Be Remembered" shows the same quality.

Lot's wife is an example of worldly-mindedness, and her tragic end is a warning to avoid giving our souls to the things of earth. First John 2:15 gives us the precept to go along with the example of Lot's wife: "Do not love the world or the things in the world."

41

Death Is the Gate of Life

LILIAS TROTTER

"Death is the Gate of Life." There was deep insight in those old words. For man's natural thought of death is that of a dreary ending in decay and dissolution. And from his standpoint he is right: death as the punishment of sin *is* an ending.

But far other is God's thought in the redemption of the world. He takes the very thing that came in with the curse, and makes it the path of glory. Death becomes a beginning instead of an ending, for it becomes the means of liberating a fresh life. And so the hope that lies in these parable lessons of death and life is meant for those only who are turning to Him for redemption. To those who have *not* turned, death stands in all its old awful doom, inevitable, irrevocable. There is no gleam of light through it for them.

"The death of the Cross"—death's triumph hour—that was the point where God's gate opened; and to that gate we come again and again, as our lives unfold, and through it pass even on earth to our joyful resurrection, to a life each time more abundant, for each time the dying is a deeper dying. The Christian life is a process of deliverance out of one world into another, and "death," as has been truly said, "is the only way out of any world in which we are."

"Death is the gate of life." Does it look so to us? Have we learnt to go down, once and again, into its gathering shadows in quietness and confidence, knowing that there is always "a better resurrection" beyond? . . .

Death is the only way out of the world of condemnation wherein we lie. Shut into that world, it is vain to try by any self-effort to battle out; nothing can revoke the decree "the soul that sinneth, it shall die." The only choice left is this. Shall it be, under the old headship of Adam, our own death, in all that God means by the word, or shall it be, under the headship of Christ, the death of another in our place?

It is when we come to self-despair, when we feel ourselves locked in, waiting our doom, that the glory and the beauty of God's way of escape dawns upon us, and we submit ourselves to Him in it. All resistance breaks down as faith closes on the fact: "He loved me and gave Himself for me." We receive the atonement so hardly won, and we go out into life not only pardoned, but cleared and justified. . . .

- Death to sin's penalty is the way out into a life of justification. . . .
- Death to sin is the way out into a life of holiness. . . .
- Death to lawful things is the way out into a life of surrender. . . .
- Death to self is the way out into a life of sacrifice. . . .

Yes, life is the uppermost, resurrection life, radiant and joyful and strong, for we represent down here Him who liveth and was dead and is alive for evermore. . . . A gateway is never a dwelling-place; the death-stage is never meant for our souls to stay and brood over, but to pass through with a will into the light beyond . . . , for above all and through all is the inflowing, overflowing life of Jesus. . . . He is not a God of the dead, but a God of the living, and He would have us let the glory of His gladness shine out.[1]

Lilias Trotter (1853–1928) was a British author, artist, and missionary to Algeria. Victorian giant John Ruskin encouraged Trotter to devote her life to painting in the belief that she could become the greatest living painter, but Trotter turned her back on that possibility and chose the life of a missionary instead. As the devotional printed here shows, Trotter was a person of evangelical conviction and fervor. According to a biographer, while on her deathbed, as attendants sang a hymn, Trotter exclaimed, "A chariot and six horses." When asked whether she was seeing beautiful things, Trotter famously replied, "Yes, many beautiful things."[2]

In the middle years of her life, Trotter published two short devotional books with interspersed drawings of plants. The titles were *Parables of the Cross* and *Parables of the Christ-Life*. The devotional printed here is taken from the first of these two books. The concept of *parables* has a double meaning here—lessons taught by Christ (who taught in parables) and also lessons learned from the plants that Trotter sketched and painted.

The excerpted material from *Parables of the Cross* focuses on an unattributed traditional saying that death is the gate of life. With that as a starting point, Trotter turns the prism of that saying in the light. The result is meditative writing at its best. Every paragraph springs a new variation on the central theme that death is the gate of life. In keeping with the other entries in this anthology, Trotter has a gift for challenging the common understanding of the chosen subject, for presenting it in a paradoxical light, and for sparking new insight. In Trotter's handling, we contemplate many nuances about death that we had not adequately considered before. Some of these ideas appear in bulleted format, and these are section headings in Trotter's book. Each one can be pondered as a devotional by itself.

Jesus's words in John 12:24–25 express the same paradox as Trotter's assertions: "Truly, truly, I say to you, unless a grain of wheat falls into the earth and dies, it remains alone; but if it dies, it bears much fruit. Whoever loves his life loses it, and whoever hates his life in this world will keep it for eternal life."

42

Three Puritan Exhortations to Remember God's Visitations

JOHN BUNYAN, RICHARD BAXTER,

AND WALTER PRINGLE

Children, Grace be with you. *Amen.* . . . I being taken from you in presence [i.e., imprisoned for twelve years for preaching] . . . yet that you may see my soul hath fatherly care and desire after your spiritual and everlasting welfare, I now . . . do look yet after you all, greatly longing to see your safe arrival into the desired Haven. . . .

It is profitable for Christians to be often calling to mind the very beginnings of grace with their souls. . . . My dear children, call to mind the former days, and years of ancient times: remember also your songs in the night, and commune with your own hearts. . . . Yea, look diligently, and leave no corner therein unsearched for that treasure hid, even the treasure of your first and second experience of the grace of God towards you. Remember, I say, the word that first laid hold upon you: remember your terrors of conscience, and fear of death and hell: remember also your tears and prayers to God; yea, how you sighed under every hedge for mercy. . . . Have you forgot . . . the milk-house, the stable, the barn, and the like, where God did visit your souls? Remember also the word, the word, I say, upon which the Lord hath caused you to hope. . . . [1]

John Bunyan (1628–1688) to his children

If thou be a Christian indeed, I know thou hast, if not in thy book, yet certainly in thy heart, a great many precious favors upon record, the very remembrance and rehearsal of them is sweet; how much more sweet was the actual enjoyment. . . . Look over the excellent mercies of thy youth and education, the mercies of riper years or age, the mercies of thy prosperity and thy adversity, the mercies of thy several places and relations; are they not excellent? Canst thou not think on the several places thou hast lived in and remember that they have each had their several mercies; the mercies of such a place and such a place; and all of them very rich and engaging mercies? . . .[2]

Richard Baxter (1615–1691) to all Christians

I was in the inner garden, praying to my God, in the time of my wife's travailing [labor], when the news of thy birth came unto me, and before I came to see my wife, or had seen thy face, I bowed down upon my knees to worship and give thanks unto God. . . . This I did at the plum tree, on the north side of the garden door; I mention the place, that (if thou come to years) it may put thee in mind, in the first moment of thy coming into the world.[3]

Walter Pringle (1625–1667) to his son

❈

The common threads in these Puritan passages merge to produce a unified devotional. Together they give us insight into important aspects of the Puritan soul, and these can be food for our own souls.

One theme is the continuity of the faith throughout our lives and from one generation to the next. Two of the passages are addressed by fathers to young children for the purpose of directing their spiritual lives when they become adults. In a similar vein, Baxter asks his adult readers to reach back to their childhood as they recall God's providential blessings in their lives. All three authors speak to us from a parent's heart.

A second theme is the need to remember God's visitations and mercies to us and to derive strength from our remembrance of them. To the Puritans, rehearsing God's dealings with us becomes an act of gratitude, praise, and assurance of our spiritual state. Puritan Richard Sibbes wrote that "if we were well read in the story of our own lives, we might have a divinity [theology] of our own, drawn out of the observations of God's particular dealing toward us."[4]

The most original contribution of these excerpts is the way in which all three authors link God's providential dealings and visitations to us with specific physical places. As we think about this, it makes total sense. When we consider the contour of our own spiritual pilgrimage, the most natural way to organize the storyline is by specific places where landmark spiritual experiences and providential events occurred.

As we observe the categories of places that the three authors single out for mention, another Puritan trait emerges, namely, the sanctity of the common. The Puritans championed the idea that the great spiritual realities are lived out in the everyday circumstances of life. In the three excerpts we read about meeting God in the milk house and barn, in the various places where we have lived, and at a plum tree near a garden door.

—⊶⊷—

The Bible is filled with commands and statements of resolve to remember what God has done. One of these passages is Psalm 77:11: "I will remember the deeds of the LORD."

43

A Believer's Last Day
Is His Best Day

THOMAS BROOKS

Believers, your dying-day is your best day! Oh, then, be not afraid of death. And to help you in this, remember that to be unwilling to die is not such a slight matter as some make it. There is much reproach cast upon God by believers being unwilling to die. You talk much of God, heaven, and glory—and yet when you should come to go and share in this glory, you shrug and say, "Spare me a little while!" Is not this a reproach to the God of glory? . . .

Remember that Christ's death is a death-conquering death. Christ has taken away the sting of death, so that it cannot hurt you. His death is a death-sanctifying and a death-sweetening death. He has by His death sanctified and sweetened death to us. . . . "Death reigned from Adam to Moses," says Paul (Rom. 5:14). Oh! But the Lord Jesus has, as it were, disarmed death and triumphed over it. He has taken away its sting, so that it cannot harm us. . . .

Consider that the saints' dying-day is to them the Lord's payday. Every prayer shall then have its answer; all hungerings and thirstings shall be filled and satisfied; every sigh, groan, and tear that has fallen from the saints' eyes shall then be recompensed. . . . Then a crown shall be set upon their heads, glorious robes

148

put upon their backs. . . . Their dying-day being the Lord's pay-day, they shall hear the Lord saying to them, "Well done, good and faithful servant . . . enter thou into the joy of thy lord" (Matt. 25:23). In that day they shall find that God . . . will make good all those golden and glorious promises that He has made to them. . . . Now God will give them gold for brass, silver for iron, felicity for misery, plenty for poverty, honor for dishonor, freedom for bondage, heaven for earth, an immortal crown for a mortal crown. . . .

Christians! what is your whole life but a day to fit for the hour of death? What is your great business in this world but to prepare and fit for the eternal world? . . . Therefore, as you love your souls—and as you would be happy in death, and everlastingly blessed after death—prepare for death! See that you build upon nothing below Christ! See that you have a real interest in Christ. . . . See that you are fruitful, faithful, and watchful.

Then your dying-day shall be to you as the day of harvest to the farmer, as the day of deliverance to the prisoner, as the day of coronation to the king, and as the day of marriage to the bride. Your dying-day shall be a day of triumph and exaltation, a day of freedom and consolation, a day of rest and satisfaction![1]

Most people think about their own death as a fearful prospect. The title of this famous Puritan funeral sermon offers a pleasing alternative: a believer's last day on earth is his or her best day. The Puritans were at their devotional "best" in the genre of funeral sermons. By the time these sermons found their way into print, they had often been expanded into a small book.

When Thomas Brooks (1608–1680) preached a sermon at the funeral of Mrs. Martha Randoll at Christ's Church, London, on June 28, 1651, he chose a title that is a stroke of genius. By calling a believer's last day on earth his or her *best day*, Brooks at once demolishes the conventional view of death as an earthly calamity. We are immediately curious about how the stated thesis can possibly be true.

Tracing Brooks's line of argument is a good way to read his words devotionally. Each of the first three paragraphs printed here develops a separate argument in support of the main idea, as we read about the ignominy of fearing death, the fact that Jesus has conquered death for a believer, and the glories that await us in heaven. The next paragraph solemnly reminds us that preparation for eternity is the chief task of earthly life, and the final paragraph is a barrage of evocative metaphors that make our day of death totally appealing to us. This Puritan sermon is a triumph of winning us to an idea that initially seems difficult to accept.

———◈◈◈———

Puritan funeral sermons took a single Bible verse as their point of departure. Brooks chose Ecclesiastes 7:1:

A good name is better than precious ointment,
   and the day of death than the day of birth.

44

Charity and Its Fruits

JONATHAN EDWARDS

Oh! what joy will there be, springing up in the hearts of the saints, after they have passed through their wearisome pilgrimage, to be brought to such a paradise as [heaven]! Here is joy unspeakable indeed, and full of glory—joy that is humble, holy, enrapturing, and divine in its perfection! Love is always a sweet principle; and especially divine love. This, even on earth, is a spring of sweetness; but in heaven it shall become a stream, a river, an ocean! All shall stand about the God of glory, who is the great fountain of love, opening, as it were, their very souls to be filled with those effusions of love that are poured forth from his fullness, just as the flowers on the earth, in the bright and joyous days of spring, open their bosoms to the sun, to be filled with his light and warmth, and to flourish in beauty and fragrancy under his cheering rays.

Every saint in heaven is as a flower in that garden of God, and holy love is the fragrance and sweet odor that they all send forth, and with which they fill the bowers of that paradise above. Every soul there is as a note in some concert of delightful music, that sweetly harmonizes with every other note, and all together blend in the most rapturous strains in praising God and the Lamb forever. . . .

Let the consideration of what has been said of heaven stir up all earnestly to seek after it. If heaven be such a blessed world, then let it be our chosen country, and the inheritance that we look for and seek. Let us turn our course this way, and press on to its possession. . . . It is offered to us. . . . If you would be in the way to the world of love, see that you live a life of love—of love to God, and love to men. All of us hope to have part in the world of love hereafter, and therefore we should cherish the spirit of love, and live a life of holy love here on earth. This is the way to be like the inhabitants of heaven, who are now confirmed in love forever. Only in this way can you be like them in excellence and loveliness, and like them, too, in happiness, and rest, and joy. By living in love in this world, you may be like them, too, in sweet and holy peace, and thus have, on earth, the foretastes of heavenly pleasures and delights. . . .

Thus, also, you may have a sense of the glory of heavenly things, as of God, and Christ, and holiness; and your heart be disposed and opened by holy love to God, and by the spirit of peace and love to men, to a sense of the excellence and sweetness of all that is to be found in heaven. Thus shall the windows of heaven be as it were opened, so that its glorious light shall shine in upon your soul. Thus you may have the evidence of your fitness for that blessed world, and that you are actually on the way to its possession.[1]

Charity and Its Fruits is a Puritan classic authored by New England preacher Jonathan Edwards (1703–1758). It is a series of sermons built around the great love chapter of the Bible (1 Corinthians 13). But the last chapter of Edwards's book, from which the selection printed here has been taken, is written in a devotional rather than expository mode. The first thing that we need to clarify is that the word *charity* was the standard term for "love" right into the twentieth century, and indeed the King James Version uses that word throughout 1 Corinthians 13.

The overall tenor of Edwards's book is what we would expect—a detailed exploration of the spiritual and moral virtue of love. How, then, do we get to a long, rapturous chapter about heaven at the conclusion of the book? Heaven is presented by Edwards as the supreme example and ultimate fulfilment of love. But this heavenly love is not only reserved for the future. What exists in perfection in heaven is part of a continuum that embraces our earthly lives as well. Edwards skillfully presents heaven as an incentive and model for living lives of love right now.

The strength of the passage is partly its lyrical and poetic form. The appeal is not primarily to our minds but to our hearts and imaginations. Edwards wrote a whole book on what he called the "religious affections" (the old word for emotions and longings), and in this passage he awakens our religious affections. Not surprisingly, the original subtitle of the book was *Christian Love as Manifested in the Heart and Life*.

Edwards made heavenly love the climax of his treatise on love. 1 Corinthians 13 ends the same way: "So faith, hope, love abide, these three; but the greatest of these is love. Make love your aim" (1 Cor. 13:13; 14:1 RSV).

45

Reflections on Providence

The Westminster Confession
and Heidelberg Catechism

Westminster Confession

God the great Creator of all things doth
    uphold, direct, dispose, and govern
all creatures, actions, and things,
    from the greatest even to the least,
by his most wise and holy providence,

according to his infallible foreknowledge,
    and the free and immutable counsel of his own will,
to the praise of the glory
    of his wisdom, power, justice, goodness, and mercy.[1]

Heidelberg Catechism

Q. 27. What do you mean by the providence of God?
A. The almighty and everywhere present power of God,
    whereby, as it were by his hand,
he still upholds heaven, earth, and all creatures,
and so governs them that herbs and grass,
    rain and drought,
    fruitful and barren years,
    food and drink,

health and sickness,
 riches and poverty,
 yea, all things,
come not by chance but by his fatherly hand.

Q. 28. What does it profit us to know that God has created, and
by his providence still upholds, all things?
A. That we may be patient in adversity,
 thankful in prosperity,
and with a view to the future
 may have good confidence in our faithful God and Father,
that no creature shall separate us from his love,
since all creatures are so in his hand
 that without his will they cannot so much as move.[2]

The doctrine of providence is a mainstay of Christian belief, and all sys-
tematic theologies devote major space to it. If we ask why the famous
formulations about providence printed here have been memorized and
remained in constant circulation for centuries, the answer does not lie
in their doctrinal content, since that is the same as the fleeting statements made in theology books. The statements from the Confession
and Catechism became classic texts by virtue of their style. They employ eloquence in the service of truth. The particular kind of eloquence
belongs to prose rather than poetry.

The primary ingredient in this prose elegance is the sentence structure
and the marshaling of phrases and clauses in linear sequence. The sentences are long and formal, with each of the three items consisting of a
single sweeping sentence. The individual units employ parallelism (as in
the four parallel verbs *uphold*, *direct*, *dispose*, and *govern*). More globally,
the clauses and phrases, even when they are not parallel in construction,
unfold in a wavelike manner. Even in silent reading, but preeminently in
oral performance, we experience the rise and fall of language, producing
a pleasing repetition. Even though the three statements are linear prose,
they have been printed here in a manner to enhance these effects.

The majesty we have been noting produces an effect of overflowing copia or abundance, fueled by an impulse to fill out the details and ramifications. We are led to feel that there is no stopping when we embark on a definition of divine providence. Nearly every element is elaborated with three, four, or more words or phrases, as if one is not enough. The energy and exuberance of style lead us to luxuriate in divine providence in a manner commensurate with the form in which it is expressed. We are swept up into *feeling* that God's providence is abundant.

If we compress the doctrine of providence to its essence, the idea of God's provision for human life emerges as the central principle. Abraham asserted this principle when God provided a ram as a substitute offering for his son Isaac: "So Abraham called the name of that place, 'The LORD will provide'" (Gen. 22:14).

46

The Pursuit of God

A. W. Tozer

When we sing, "Draw me nearer, nearer, blessed Lord," we are not thinking of the nearness of place, but of the nearness of relationship. It is for increasing degrees of awareness that we pray, for a more perfect consciousness of the divine Presence. . . . Why do some persons "find" God in a way that others do not? . . . I venture to suggest that the one vital quality which they had in common was *spiritual receptivity*. Something in them was open to heaven, something which urged them Godward. Without attempting anything like a profound analysis I shall say simply that they had spiritual awareness and that they went on to cultivate it until it became the biggest thing in their lives. They differed from the average person in that when they felt the inward longing they *did something about it*. They acquired the lifelong habit of spiritual response. . . .

Receptivity is not a single thing; it is a compound rather, a blending of several elements within the soul. It is an affinity for, a bent toward, a sympathetic response to, a desire to have. From this it may be gathered that it can be present in degrees, that we may have little or more or less, depending upon the individual. It may be increased by exercise or destroyed by neglect. . . . It is a gift of God, indeed, but one which must be recognized and cultivated as any other gift if it is to realize the purpose for which it was given. . . .

Let us say it again: The Universal Presence is a fact. God is here. The whole universe is alive with His life. And He is no strange or foreign God, but the familiar Father of our Lord Jesus Christ whose love has for these thousands of years enfolded the sinful race of men. And always He is trying to get our attention, to reveal Himself to us, to communicate with us. We have within us the ability to know Him if we will but respond to His overtures. (And this we call pursuing God!) We will know Him in increasing degree as our receptivity becomes more perfect by faith and love and practice.

A spiritual kingdom lies all about us, enclosing us, embracing us, altogether within reach of our inner selves, waiting for us to recognize it. God Himself is here waiting our response to His Presence. This eternal world will come alive to us the moment we begin to reckon upon its reality. . . . If we truly want to follow God we must seek to be other-worldly. . . . But we must avoid the common fault of pushing the "other world" into the future. It is not future, but present. It parallels our familiar physical world, and the doors between the two worlds are open.[1]

The Pursuit of God, the best known book by Aiden Wilson Tozer (1897–1963), is one of the most famous devotional books in modern times. Today it is available in print editions offered by a dozen different publishers, supplemented by online texts and audio versions. A panel of magazine editors called the book one of the all-time most inspirational books. What accounts for this appeal?

Tozer, a pastor and author affiliated with the Christian and Missionary Alliance denomination, was a plainspoken man who even chose not to own a car despite his public prominence. His style is simple and straightforward, so we need to look to his message to see what raises his book to the status of a classic.

The very subject of pursuing or seeking God strikes at the heart of the human situation. As Augustine pinpointed, God made people for himself, so their bent is to seek him. But Tozer implicitly challenges the conventional view of how this works. When we speak of pursuing someone, we most naturally think of needing to undertake a strenuous search operation to find a distant or hidden or elusive person. Tozer's paradoxical view is that God is everywhere around us, so we don't need to search at all. Tozer himself signals the surprise element in all this in an ironic parenthetical sentence that reads, *And this we call pursuing God!* In other words, what we call pursuing God is not a pursuit as we ordinarily view it, but rather an act of recognition and then a relating to God when we see him. But for this to happen, we need to embrace the unseen spiritual world by faith.

Tozer strikes just the right balance between making us see that drawing closer to God is within the reach of every earnest seeker, and on the other hand convicting us that we should be doing more to draw close to God than we ordinarily do.

The logic underlying Tozer's message is that God and the spiritual world are as real as the physical world around us, but it requires faith to live according to this premise. Hebrews 11:6 asserts the same truth: "And without faith it is impossible to please [God], for whoever would draw near to God must believe that he exists and that he rewards those who seek him."

47

The Care of the Soul Urged as the One Thing Needful

GEORGE WHITEFIELD

My friends, the words [spoken by Jesus] which are now before us, are this day as true as they were seventeen hundred years ago. Set your hearts to attend to them, that you may, by divine grace, be awakened to hear them with a due regard and be so impressed with the plain and serious things which are now to be spoken, as you probably would if I were speaking by your dying beds, and you had the near and lively view of eternity. . . .

The care of the soul implies a readiness to hear the words of Christ. . . . It supposes that we learn from this divine teacher the worth of our souls, their danger, and their remedy; and that we become above all things solicitous about their salvation. That, heartily repenting of all our sins, and cordially believing the everlasting gospel, we receive the Lord Jesus Christ for righteousness and life, resting our souls on the value of his atonement, and the efficacy of his grace. . . . This is the "one thing needful. . . ."

How necessary is it that we should seriously inquire how this one thing needful is regarded by us. Let me entreat you to remember your own concern in it, and inquire, Have I thought seriously of it? Have I seen the importance of it? Has it lain with a due and abiding weight on my mind? Has it brought me to Christ, that I might lay the stress of these great eternal interests on him? . . . Am I willing, in fact, to give up other things, my interests, my pleasures, my passions to this? . . .

I would in the last place address myself to those happy souls who have in good earnest attended to the one thing needful. I hope, that when you see how commonly it is neglected, neglected indeed, by many, whose natural capacities, improvements, and circumstances in life appear to you superior to your own, you will humbly acknowledge that it was distinguishing grace which brought you into this happy state, and formed you to this most necessary care. Bless the Lord, therefore, who hath given you that counsel. . . .

Remember still to endeavor to continue acting on these great principles, which at first determined your choice. . . . Being enabled to secure the great concern, make yourselves easy as to others of smaller importance. You have chosen the kingdom of God, and his righteousness; other things, therefore, shall be added unto you: and if any which you desire should not be added, comfort yourselves with this thought, that you have the good part, which can never be taken away. And . . . be very solicitous that others may be brought to a care about the one thing needful. If it be needful for you, it is so for your children, your friends, your servants. Let them, therefore, see your concern in this respect for them, as well as for yourselves. Let parents especially attend to this exhortation; whose care for their offspring often exceeds in other respects, and falls in this. . . .

May this grand care be awakened in those by whom it has been hitherto neglected: may it be revived in each of our minds. . . . If you commit this precious jewel [your soul], which is your eternal all, into his hand, he will preserve it unto that day, and will then produce it richly adorned, and gloriously improved to his own honor, and to your everlasting joy.[1]

George Whitefield (1714–1770) is one of the most famous evangelistic preachers in the history of Christendom. It is estimated that he preached some eighteen thousand times, and his ability to be heard by multitudes without the aid of loud-speaking equipment is legendary.[2] He was a leading figure of the Great Awakening in the American colonies. We naturally wonder what his preaching was like. The excerpt printed here provides answers.

First, Whitefield awakens in his listeners and readers a sense of the momentous importance of what he is proclaiming. The very topic of his sermon on the *one* thing needful sounds this keynote, but beyond that, Whitefield continuously conveys a sense that his message is a life-or-death matter.

In addition to this tone of urgency, a firm logic underlies Whitefield's train of thought. In his message about the one thing needful, Whitefield systematically tells us (a) what the thing needful is, (b) why it is of utmost importance that we give it priority, and (c) how we can go about giving it that priority. What, why, and how: it is a message easily grasped, complete in coverage, and winsome in its simplicity.

A final technique in Whitefield's rhetorical arsenal is his stance of direct address to his listeners and readers. We cannot fail to notice how many times he addresses us directly, often in the form of commands. The persuasive effect is to leave us convicted of the need to do as Whitefield urges.

Whitefield's meditation on the one thing needful is based on the story of Mary and Martha narrated in Luke 10:38–42. When Martha was "distracted with much serving" (v. 40) as Mary "sat at the Lord's feet and listened to his teaching" (v. 39), Jesus commended Mary for recognizing that "one thing is necessary" (v. 42).

48

Edification from Last Wills and Testaments

WILLIAM SHAKESPEARE, MR. JUSTICE PARK, AND ROBERT KEAYNE

In the name of God, Amen. I William Shakespeare of Stratford upon Avon in the county of Warwickshire, in perfect health and memory, God be praised, do make and ordain this my last will and testament in manner and form following. That is to say first, I commend my Soul into the hands of God my Creator, hoping and assuredly believing through the only merits of Jesus Christ my Savior to be made partaker of life everlasting. And my body to the earth whereof it is made.[1]

William Shakespeare
1564–1616

In the name of the blessed and glorious Trinity, Amen. . . . I humbly recommend my soul to Almighty God, relying for my eternal salvation on the sole merits and all perfect atonement of my blessed Lord and Savior Jesus Christ, on my sincere contrition and repentance. . . .

I desire that my body may be decently buried at as small an expense as possible consistent with the respect due to my deserving family, leaving all arrangements as to place and manner to my beloved executors. . . .

Having now made the best and most equitable disposition in my power of the worldly wealth with which it has pleased a gracious God to bless me, . . . I heartily and devoutly pray (in this moment of serious thought) that the Almighty may shower down upon my children and my dear grandchildren his heavenly blessing.

And now in peace and charity with all mankind, grateful to God for his unbounded mercies, . . . for excellent and virtuous friends, for affectionate and dutiful children, and for more than forty years of conjugal happiness with the best of women, I conclude this will, trusting in the Divine Mercy for the forgiveness of all my offenses for the merits and atonement of my only Lord and Savior.[2]

Mr. Justice Park
will dated 1836

Considering that all flesh is as grass that must wither and will return to the dust and that my life may be taken away in a moment, therefore that I may be in the better readiness, . . . I do now in my health make, ordain, and declare this to be my last will and testament. . . .

First and before all things, I commend and commit my precious soul into the hands of Almighty God, who not only as a loving creator hath given it unto me, . . . but also as a most loving father and merciful savior hath redeemed it with the precious blood of His own dear son and my sweet Jesus from that gulf of misery and ruin that I by original sin and actual transgressions had plunged it into. . . . I look for my acceptance with God and the salvation of my soul only from the merits or righteousness of the Lord Jesus Christ, and from the free, bountiful, and undeserved grace and love of God in Him. . . .

This being premised in respect of my soul and my faith in Jesus Christ, I do next commit my body to the earth (and to comely and decent burial), there to rest till my loving Savior by His almighty power shall raise it up again, at which time I confidently believe it shall be reunited to my own soul.[3]

Robert Keayne
1595–1656

The devotional potential of these excerpts from last wills and testaments keeps expanding as we give ourselves to pondering them. All three statements date to earlier eras when it was a standard practice to include statements of personal testimony in a will. The first passage is the preamble to the will of William Shakespeare, the most famous English literary author of all time. By contrast, all that we know about the author of the second passage is his name, his profession (judge), and a friend's description of him as "a pious layman." Robert Keayne was a prosperous Boston businessman of the Puritan era.

Several old meditative traditions provide a context for assimilating these printed passages devotionally. Through the centuries (and especially in the Middle Ages), contemplating one's death has been a standard meditative practice. Secondly, a person's final or dying words have always been considered important, especially to family members. And thirdly, statements of personal testimony have been a significant part of Christian life in community. All of these elements are present in the specimens of what past eras quaintly called "testimonial acts."

Most of the devotional classics collected in this anthology have the quality of being a statement of first things, calling us back to what is most important in our spiritual lives. All three of the authors quoted here took time to formulate in their minds what is *the* most important thing in life, and they all agree on what it is. These passages do not cover the whole of the Christian life but focus on what it will be like when earthly life is over and we stand individually before God. These carefully worded statements can aid us in preparing for our own deaths.

This composite meditation on death clarifies the way in which Christians reside in two worlds. One world is spiritual and eternal, and the preambles to the wills assert the primacy of the spiritual. But we are also physical and earthly creatures, and the passages lead us to ponder that in helpful ways as well. Our bodies will be buried, and we need to face that. We have families and friends who will be sorrowing survivors, and we need to picture that. There will be a funeral service for us. The more we analyze what is going on in these passages, the more strength we can derive from them as a meditation on our own death and immortality. This meditation on first things is paradoxically also a meditation on last things.

The moving spirit behind all three final statements is the principle encapsulated in Hebrews 9:27 that "it is appointed for man to die once, and after that comes judgment."

All Things Shall Be Well

JULIAN OF NORWICH

In my darkness, crying to God, the light came first as by a soft general dawning of comfort for faith. *"Sin is inevitable* [in a fallen world], *but all shall be well, and all manner of things shall be well."* But I thought, "Ah good Lord, how might all be well, in view of the great hurt that is come by sin to the creature?"

The answer . . . is that . . . grace works our dreadful failing into plenteous, endless solace, and grace works our shameful falling into high, worshipful rising; and grace works our sorrowful dying into holy, blissful life. . . . And out of the tender love that our good Lord has to all that shall be saved, He comforts readily and sweetly, signifying [that] *all shall be well, and all manner* [of] *things shall be well.* . . . And in these words we can see a marvelous and high mystery hid in God, which mystery He shall openly make known to us in Heaven, in which knowing we shall verily see the cause why He allowed sin to come, in which sight we shall endlessly joy in our Lord God. . . . God wills that we take heed to these words, and that we be ever strong in sure trust, in weal and woe. For He loves and enjoys us, and so wills He that we love and enjoy Him and mightily trust in Him; and *all shall be well.* . . .

All shall be well. For the fulness of joy is to behold God in *all.* By the same blessed Might, Wisdom, and Love that He made all things, to the same end our good Lord leads continually, and

thereto He shall bring it; and when it is time we shall see it. . . .
He wills that we know that He takes heed not only to noble and
great things, but also to little and small, to low and to simple. . . .
And therefore He says that all manner of things shall be well. For
He wishes us to know that the least thing shall not be forgotten.

Another understanding [of the claim that all shall be well]
is that there are deeds of evil done in our sight, and such great
harms taken, that it seems to us that it were impossible that it
should ever come to a good end. And upon this we look, sorrowing and mourning, so that we cannot resign ourselves to the
blissful beholding of God as we should. . . . Thus in these [words
that all shall be well] I understand a mighty comfort of all the
works of our Lord God that are yet to come. There is a Deed
the which the blessed Trinity shall do in the last Day, and when
the Deed shall be, and how it shall be done, is unknown of all
creatures that are beneath Christ, and shall be till it is done. . . .
This is that Great Deed ordained of our Lord God from without
beginning, treasured and hid in His blessed breast, only known
to Himself: by which He shall make all things well. For just as
the blissful Trinity made all things out of nothing, so the same
blessed Trinity shall make well all that is not well.[1]

In the annals of devotional writing, some authors are inseparably
linked in our minds to a famous aphorism or saying that belongs to
them. We automatically associate Augustine with his statement that
our souls are restless till they rest in God, and the Westminster Shorter
Catechism with the principle that our chief end is to glorify God and
enjoy him forever. Julian of Norwich (1343–1416) is famous to the
world on the strength of her aphorism that *all shall be well*. We might
note in passing that it was the modern English poet T. S. Eliot who gave
the aphorism currency. Until Eliot incorporated it into his poem *Little
Gidding*, it was relatively unknown.[2]

Julian of Norwich (not her real name, which is unknown) was an
anchoress—someone who lived in her cell and devoted herself to prayer

and contemplation. At the age of thirty, Julian fell seriously ill, and all around her thought she was on her deathbed. In this state, she received sixteen visions from God. She did not die, and when she revived, she wrote the visions down. Then a quarter of a century later she subjected her visions to theological analysis. The important thing about Julian's statement that *all shall be well* is that she did not compose the statement but received it as a vision.

We find the famous aphorism immediately captivating and memorable, but then upon reflection we cannot help wondering how this optimistic statement can possibly be true, or in what ways it can be true. Wonder of wonders, Julian was also baffled by the saying! Over the course of three chapters in her book, she intermittently circles back to the revelation that she received and subjects it to analysis. We can read the successive paragraphs printed here as recording stages of discovery and increasing understanding. As we follow Julian's pathway of discovery, we experience the revelation as she did, namely, as a statement of faith in God and his good purposes for those who place their trust in him.

Before we leave the aphorism about all things being well, we should admire a nuance of its artistry. The statement would not possess the same voltage without the element of parallelism. The aphorism follows the same pattern as climactic parallelism in the Bible, where the second line repeats part of the first line and then adds to it. In this instance, *all manner of things* is the added element. We experience it as an intensification of the original statement but are also prompted to ponder how this added element adds to the overall meaning of the statement. Throughout the entire passage, the words are beautiful and laden with religious feeling.

As we ponder Julian of Norwich's famous saying, our minds inevitably make a connection to Romans 8:28: "And we know that for those who love God all things work together for good, for those who are called according to his purpose."

169

50

Knowing God

J. I. Packer

What is a Christian? The question can be answered in many ways, but the richest answer I know is that a Christian is one who has God as Father. . . . You sum up the whole of New Testament *teaching* in a single phrase, if you speak of it as a revelation of the Fatherhood of the holy Creator. In the same way, you sum up the whole of New Testament *religion* if you describe it as the knowledge of God as one's holy Father. If you want to judge how well a person understands Christianity, find out how much he makes of the thought of being God's child, and having God as his Father. If this is not the thought that prompts and controls his worship and prayers and his whole outlook on life, it means that he does not understand Christianity very well at all. . . . "Father" is the Christian name for God. . . .

The immediate message to our hearts of what [has just been said] is surely this: Do I, as a Christian, understand myself? Do I know my own real identity? My own real destiny? I am a child of God. God is my Father; heaven is my home; every day is one day nearer. My Savior is my brother; every Christian is my brother too. Say it over and over to yourself. . . . For this is the Christian's secret of—a happy life?—yes, certainly, but we have something both higher and profounder to say. This is the Christian's secret of a *Christian* life, and of a *God-honoring* life, and these are the aspects of the situation that really matter. . . .

To help us realize more adequately who and what, as children of God, we are and are called to be, here are some questions by which we do well to examine ourselves again and again.
Do I understand my adoption? Do I value it? Do I daily remind myself of my privilege as a child of God? . . .

Do I treat God as my Father in heaven, loving, honoring and
obeying him, seeking and welcoming his fellowship and trying
in everything to please him, as a human parent would want his
child to do?

Do I think of Jesus Christ, my Savior and my Lord, as my
brother too, bearing to me not only a divine authority but also
a divine-human sympathy? Do I think daily how close he is to
me, how completely he understands me, and how much as my
kinsman-redeemer, he cares for me?

Have I learned to hate the things that displease my Father?
Am I sensitive to the evil things to which he is sensitive? Do I
make a point of avoiding them, lest I grieve him? . . .

Am I proud of my Father, and of his family, to which by his
grace I belong?

Does the family likeness appear in me? If not, why not?

God humble us; God instruct us; God make us his own true
children.[1]

Although J. I. Packer (1926–2020) was so prolific that it is impossible to compile a complete bibliography of his writings, *Knowing
God* is decisively the book that made him a famous author.[2] Packer
is the common person's theologian, and his signature book runs true
to form in this regard. The book was born when the editor of a small
British evangelical magazine asked Packer to write a series of articles
on the subject of God. The articles unfolded over a five-year span, and
before composing each one, Packer asked himself, "What shall I tell
them next?"

The first key to assimilating the passage is to link it to the book's
title. Packer does not do this explicitly, but we ourselves can do it:
knowing God means living in an awareness that God is our father, and

that we are his children. It is as simple as that. We can see that Packer avoids theological abstraction and instead incarnates knowledge of God in terms of the parent-child metaphor. The entire passage has a metaphoric understructure. And in keeping with the general tenor of the passages in this anthology, there is a surprise element: How many of us would define the essence of Christianity in terms of the father-child metaphor?

Packer was a modern-day Puritan, and this passage illustrates it perfectly. It shows the practical bent of Puritanism, as Packer is not content with exposition of his core idea but goes on to list a series of questions of self-diagnosis. The listing technique is a signature Puritan strategy, and as the list unfolds, it acquires a convicting quality, prompting us to what the Puritans called a holy reformation of our lives.

─── ❦ ───

Packer's claim that New Testament Christianity makes much of the idea that believers have been adopted by God as their Father finds confirmation in 1 John 3:1: "See what kind of love the Father has given to us, that we should be called children of God; and so we are."

Notes on Sources

Editor's Introduction

1. T. S. Eliot's statement about how literary authors overcome the cliché effect of what is overly familiar by dislocating language into meaning was made in his essay on the metaphysical poets: *Selected Essays* (London: Faber and Faber, 1932), 289.
2. Ralph Waldo Emerson's comments about the poet as sent into the world for the purpose of expression appears in his essay "The Poet," reprinted in *Major Writers of America*, ed. Perry Miller (New York: Harcourt, Brace, and World, 1962), 1:530–31.

Devotional 1: Finding Rest for Our Restless Heart (Augustine)

1. Augustine worked on his *Confessions* over a four-year span, ending in 401. The work circulated in manuscript form until being published in the late fifteenth century. The translation used for the selection is E. B. Pusey's translation (London: J. G. and R. Rivington, 1838), lightly modernized by the editor of this anthology. Although most internet sites translate Augustine's famous formula as "our hearts are restless," Augustine wrote "our heart is restless."

Devotional 2: How Jesus Is Our Hero (Gerard Manley Hopkins)

1. The passage is taken from *Gerard Manley Hopkins: Sermons and Devotional Writings*, ed. Christopher Devlin (Oxford: Oxford University Press, 1959), 34–38.

Devotional 3: Exhortation to Christlike Living (Florence Nightingale)

1. The excerpts from *Florence Nightingale to Her Nurses* are taken from the first published edition (London: Macmillan and Company,

1914). The subtitle explains the nature of the book: *A Selection of Miss Nightingale's Addresses to Probationers and Nurses of the Nightingale School at St. Thomas's Hospital.*

2. Multiple internet sites quote Nightingale's statement that "Christ is the author of our profession," including this one: https://opentheword.org.

Devotional 4: For Whom the Bell Tolls (John Donne)

1. The excerpt from Meditation 17 in *Devotions upon Emergent Occasions* is taken from *The Works of John Donne* (London: John W. Parker, 1839), 3:574–75.

Devotional 5: Communing with God through Nature (George Washington Carver)

1. The passage by Carver, as well as the material related to him in the editor's commentary, comes from *George Washington Carver in His Own Words*, ed. Gary R. Kremer (Columbia: University of Missouri Press, 1987), specifically the chapter titled "The Scientist as Mystic: Reading God out of Nature's Book" (pp. 138–43). Reprinted with the permission of University of Missouri Press.

Devotional 6: Preface to Galatians (Martin Luther)

1. The text used here is the first English translation (1575), performed by "divers learned, godly men" who wished to remain anonymous.

2. Luther's claim that Galatians was "my epistle" was originally recorded in Luther's table talks and today appears on numerous internet sites.

3. The anecdotal data about Charles Wesley and John Bunyan is well known and appears among other places in the introductory material of Martin Luther, *Galatians*, ed. Alister McGrath and J. I. Packer, Crossway Classic Commentary (Wheaton, IL: Crossway, 1998).

Devotional 7: Waiting on God (Andrew Murray)

1. The excerpt is taken from the first edition of *Waiting on God* (New York: Fleming Revell, 1896), 17–20, 24.

Devotional 8: The Foundational Principles of the Christian Life (The Westminster and Heidelberg Catechisms)

1. The Westminster Shorter Catechism was first published in 1647 and the Heidelberg Catechism in 1563.

2. The C. S. Lewis quotation can be found in *Reflections on the Psalms* (London: Geoffrey Bless, 1958), 4.

Devotional 9: The Imitation of Christ (Thomas à Kempis)

1. The passage from *The Imitation of Christ* is taken from the translation of William Bentham (1831–1910), which is available on multiple public domain websites. The text has been lightly modernized by the editor of this anthology. Most editions and websites devoted to this work repeat the claim that this book is the most widely printed and translated book next to the Bible.

Devotional 10: Two Prayers (Samuel Johnson)

1. From *Prayers and Meditations* (London: Vernor, Hood, and Sharpe, 1806), 117–18, 185. The claim that Psalm 51 may have been a model for Johnson's prayers rests on the fact that Johnson's petition that God not take his Holy Spirit from him appears regularly in his prayers.

2. Milton's claim that Christian poetry has the ability "to set the affections in right tune" appears in his *Reason of Church Government* (1642).

Devotional 11: Jesus Our Guide and Guardian (John Henry Newman)

1. The devotion titled "Jesus Our Guide and Guardian" is taken from Newman's *Meditations and Devotions* (London: Longmans, Green, and Company, 1893), 198–99.

Devotional 12: Bidding Prayer (Lessons and Carols)

1. A forerunner of the 1918 Lessons and Carols can be dated back to a 1880 festival of lessons and carols based on ancient sources. The author of the 1918 bidding prayer was Eric Milner-White, dean of the chapel at King's College, Cambridge. The text of the bidding prayer used in this anthology is taken from a public domain website.

Devotional 13: True and Substantial Wisdom (John Calvin)

1. Calvin's *Institutes of the Christian Religion* was first published in Latin in 1536 and first translated into English in 1561. The translation used in this anthology is by John Allen (Philadelphia, PA:

Presbyterian Board of Publications, 1831), 1:47, 49–50. The precedents of Calvin's opening sentence are noted by Ford Lewis Battles, *Institution of the Christian Religion* (Atlanta: John Knox, 1975), 327–28.

2. The quotation that the opening sentence can be contemplated for a lifetime comes from Derek Thomas, "An Intro to the Institutes," *Reformation 21*, February 10, 2017, https://www.reformation21.org.

Devotional 14: What Christians Believe (The Apostles' Creed)

1. The quoted statement about the literary excellence of the Apostles' Creed appears unattributed on some two hundred internet sites, but thanks to search engines, its source has finally been identified: Philip Schaff, *History of the Apostolic Church* (New York: Charles Scribner, 1859), 568.

Devotional 15: Following the Steps of the Master (Harriet Beecher Stowe)

1. The entry from Harriet Beecher Stowe comes from the first edition of her book *Footsteps of the Master* (New York: J. B. Ford and Company, 1877).

2. The Lincoln quotation is part of the lore surrounding Stowe, and its veracity is today so much debated that it constitutes a scholarly "cottage industry." In a web article, Daniel R. Vollaro claims that "of all the biographical details currently in circulation about Stowe, this anecdote certainly ranks among the most well known, and one finds some version of Lincoln's greeting employed in hundreds of articles, books, reviews, and Web summaries." Vollaro, "Lincoln, Stowe, and the 'Little Woman/Great War' Story: The Making, and Breaking, of a Great American Anecdote," *Journal of the Abraham Lincoln Association* 30, no. 1 (Winter 2009): 18–34, http://hdl .handle.net/2027/spo.2629860.0030.104.

Devotional 16: A Serious Call to a Devout and Holy Life (William Law)

1. The excerpts are taken from the first edition of *A Serious Call to a Devout and Holy Life* (London: William Innys, 1729), 3–4, 32.

2. William Shakespeare, *Romeo and Juliet*, X.ii.

Devotional 17: Practicing the Presence of God (Brother Lawrence)

1. The passage is taken from *The Practice of the Presence of God* (New York: Fleming H. Revell, 1895). Archaic language and punctuation have been modernized by the editor of this anthology. The translator is unidentified, with the information on the title page limited to "translated from the French."

Devotional 18: The Saints' Everlasting Rest (Richard Baxter)

1. Baxter's most famous devotional book was first published in 1650. The passage in this anthology is taken from an edition published in Charlestown, MA, by Samuel T. Armstrong in 1811, pages 155, 289, 308, 318. Some archaic stylistic features have been modernized.
2. The C. S. Lewis quotation is from *Mere Christianity* (New York: Macmillan, 1958), 104.

Devotional 19: What Makes the Bible the Greatest Book (Samuel Taylor Coleridge)

1. Samuel Taylor Coleridge's *Confessions of an Inquiring Spirit* was first published in 1834. The excerpt in this anthology is taken from an edition published in London in 1892 by Cassell and Company.

Devotional 20: Holy Living (Jeremy Taylor)

1. Excerpts were gleaned from Jeremy Taylor, *The Rule and Exercises of Holy Living* (Philadelphia, PA: J. W. Bradley, 1860), 28–36.

Devotional 21: Earthly and Divine Beauty (Jonathan Edwards)

1. The first two paragraphs are taken from "Covenant of Redemption: Excellency of Christ" (first published in 1738). The third and fourth paragraphs are from Edwards's famous treatise *The Nature of True Virtue* (published posthumously in 1765). The final paragraph is from a sermon titled "The True Christian's Life, a Journey towards Heaven," as printed in *The Works of President Edwards* (New York: Leavitt and Allen 1852), 4:575.

Devotional 22: Morning Prayer (Book of Common Prayer)

1. The passage is taken from *Book of Common Prayer* (New York: Prayer Book Society, 1865).

2. The oft-quoted aphorism from Aristophanes that "high thoughts must have high language" comes from lines 1058–59 of his play *Frogs*.

Devotional 23: Reflections on the Supreme Loveliness of Christ

1. The statement by Russian novelist Fyodor Dostoyevsky appears in a letter published in *Letters of Fyodor Michailovitch Dostoevsky to His Family and Friends*, trans. Ethel Golburn Mayne (London: Chatto & Windus, 1914), 66.
2. Jonathan Edwards's *Personal Narrative* appears on multiple public domain sites such as Early America's Digital Archives.
3. Thomas Watson's sermon "The Loveliness of Christ" appears on multiple public domain sites such as http://www.gracegems.org.
4. The anecdote involving Tennyson was originally published in the *Times*, October 13, 1892, and then reprinted in *The Puritan: An Illustrated Magazine for Free Churchmen* (London: J. Bowden, 1899), 222.

Devotional 24: On Loving God (Bernard of Clairvaux)

1. The public domain translation used for the excerpt from *On Loving God* is by an unidentified nineteenth-century translator whose translation appears on numerous internet sites.

Devotional 25: The Rare Jewel of Christian Contentment (Jeremiah Burroughs)

1. Excerpts are taken from *The Rare Jewel of Christian Contentment* (London: W. Bentley for L. Sadler and R. Beaumont, 1651).

Devotional 26: Nature as God's Signpost (Nathaniel Hawthorne)

1. Excerpts are taken from *The American Notebooks of Nathaniel Hawthorne*, ed. Sophia Hawthorne (New York: Houghton, Mifflin, and Company, 1883).
2. Joseph Schwartz is the literary scholar who made the statements about Hawthorne's religious orientation, in *American Classics Reconsidered: A Christian Appraisal*, ed. Harold C. Gardiner (New York: Charles Scribner's Sons, 1958), 126–27.

Devotional 27: Thoughts on the Mission and Greatness of Jesus (Blaise Pascal)

1. The excerpts from *Pensées* are taken from *The Thoughts of Blaise Pascal*, trans. C. Kegan Paul (London: George Bell and Sons, 1901).

Devotional 28: Holy Dying (Jeremy Taylor)

1. Excerpts are reprinted from *Rule and Exercises of Holy Dying* (London: Edward Martin, 1651), 48–58.

Devotional 29: Trusting and Praising God in Extremity (William Bradford)

1. The passage, with modernizing touches by the editor of this anthology, is taken from *History of Plimoth Plantation* (Boston: Wright and Potter, 1898), 94–97.

Devotional 30: Evening Prayer (Jane Austen)

1. Jane Austen's three evening prayers are in the public domain and available on such websites as Wikisource and in print books such as Rachel Dodge's *Praying with Jane* (Minneapolis: Bethany House, 2018). Information about Austen and her prayers was taken from this book.

Devotional 31: What the Bible Means to a Believer (The Geneva Bible and King James Version)

1. The preface to the Geneva Bible and "the translators to the reader" of the King James Version are reprinted from online public domain sites.

Devotional 32: The Almost Christian (John Wesley)

1. John Wesley's 1741 sermon was first published in 1759 in *Forty-Four Sermons*. It is available on multiple public domain websites, and the version printed in this anthology is taken from one of these.
2. A Methodist web forum board invited comment on Wesley's sermon under the rubric, "Wesley's Most Famous Sermon: What Do You Think about It?" accessed November 10, 2020, http://www.gracecentered.com.

Devotional 33: The Estate of Marriage (Martin Luther)

1. The edition used for the passage printed in this anthology is *Luther's Works*, trans. Walther I. Brandt, vol. 45 (Philadelphia, PA: Muhlenberg Press, 1962), 38–40; permission to reprint was granted by Augsburg/Fortress Press.
2. The quotation summarizing Luther's view of domestic life as a calling is from Gustaf Wingren, *Luther on Vocation*, trans. Carl C. Rasmussen (Philadelphia, PA: Muhlenberg Press, 1957), 5.

Devotional 34: Death as a Welcome Sleep (John Donne)

1. The entry from Donne's sermon is taken from *The Works of John Donne*, ed. Henry Alford (London: John W. Parker, 1839), 5:622–23.

Devotional 35: Morning and Evening (Charles Spurgeon)

1. Spurgeon's morning and evening devotionals were first published in 1866 and 1868; the selections for July 9 are from a public domain website.
2. The information from Spurgeon's autobiography is taken from *The Autobiography of Charles H. Spurgeon: 1856–1878* (Chicago: Fleming H. Revell, 1899), 316–17.

Devotional 36: The Mystery of Providence (John Flavel)

1. The book that became known by the title *The Mystery of Providence* was first published in 1678 under the title *Divine Conduct or the Mystery of Providence Opened*. The excerpts brought together to form the entry in this anthology are from *Divine Conduct: or, The Mystery of Providence* (London: W. Bayes and Son, 1820).
2. The references to *Paradise Lost* are as follows: After announcing in his opening invocation that he has taken his primary story material from Genesis 1–3, Milton alerts his readers how he will handle that subject, namely, that he will "assert eternal providence, / And justify the ways of God to men" (*Paradise Lost*, 1:25–26). As Adam and Eve leave Paradise at the end of the story, we read that "the world was all before them, where to choose / Their place of rest, and providence their guide" (*Paradise Lost*, 12:646–647). Edition used: John Milton, *Paradise Lost*, ed. William Kerrigan, et al. (New York: Modern Library, 2007).

Devotional 37: The Believer's New Name (George MacDonald)

1. The excerpt is taken from a sermon by this title in *Unspoken Sermons* (London: Alexander Strahan, 1867), 38. Archaic constructions have been modestly updated.
2. The C. S. Lewis quotation comes from *George MacDonald: An Anthology* (London: Geoffrey Bles, 1946), 30.

Devotional 38: Reflections on Mortality and Immortality (Prayer Book's Burial Service)

1. The *Book of Common Prayer* (also familiarly known as the *Prayer Book*) was first published in 1549. There have been many revisions through the centuries. The passage reprinted in this anthology is taken from *Book of Common Prayer* (New York: Prayer Book Society, 1865).

Devotional 39: The World as the Theater of God's Glory (John Calvin)

1. Excerpts are from *Institutes of the Christian Religion*, trans. John Allen (Philadelphia, PA: Presbyterian Board of Publications, 1813), 1:68, 84, 211–12, 865–66.

Devotional 40: Holiness (J. C. Ryle)

1. J. C. Ryle's signature book *Holiness* was first published in 1879. It is available today in multiple print versions and on multiple public domain websites.
2. J. I. Packer's endorsement of the Banner of Truth Trust edition can be accessed at "Holiness," Banner of Truth, accessed January 11, 2022, https://banneroftruth.org/us.

Devotional 41: Death Is the Gate of Life (Lilias Trotter)

1. The excerpts for this entry are taken from *Parables of the Cross*, first published in London in 1895 by Marschall Brothers. Excerpts for the selection in this anthology are taken from that edition.
2. The deathbed quotation is part of the lore surrounding the life of Trotter; one source among many is Miriam Huffman Rockness, *A Passion for the Impossible: The Life of Lilias Trotter* (Grand Rapids, MI: Discovery House, 2003), 324.

Devotional 42: Three Puritan Exhortations to Remember God's Visitations

1. The passage from John Bunyan comes from the opening of *Grace Abounding to the Chief of Sinners* (London: George Larkin, 1666).
2. The Richard Baxter excerpt is from *The Saints' Everlasting Rest*, in *The Practical Works of Richard Baxter* (London: George Virtue, 1836), 3:322–23.

3. The Walter Pringle passage is from *Memoirs of Walter Pringle of Greenknow* (Glasgow: John Robinson, 1739), 25.
4. The Richard Sibbes quotation is reprinted from Leland Ryken, *Worldly Saints: The Puritans as They Really Were* (Grand Rapids, MI: Zondervan, 1986), 209.

Devotional 43: A Believer's Last Day Is His Best Day (Thomas Brooks)

1. Excerpts have been gleaned from throughout the sermon printed in *The Complete Works of Thomas Brooks* (Edinburgh: James Nichol, 1866), 394–408.

Devotional 44: Charity and Its Fruits (Jonathan Edwards)

1. The selection is taken from *Charity and Its Fruits* (New York: Robert Carter and Brothers, 1854), 505–06, 521, 528–29.

Devotional 45: Reflections on Providence (The Westminster Confession and Heidelberg Catechism)

1. The definition of providence from the Westminster Confession (1648) comes from chapter 5.
2. The Heidelberg Catechism was first published in 1563.

Devotional 46: The Pursuit of God (A. W. Tozer)

1. The excerpts are taken from the first edition (Harrisburg, PA: Christian Publications, 1948). Reprinted with permission from Moody Christian Publications.

Devotional 47: The Care of the Soul Urged as the One Thing Needful (George Whitefield)

1. The source is a sermon by this title printed in *The Works of the Reverend George Whitefield* (London: Edward and Charles Dilly, 1771), 5:457–58, 473–74.
2. The claim that Whitefield preached eighteen thousand times is repeated so universally in biographical articles (including ones on internet sites) that it can be regarded as the received view on the subject.

Devotional 48: Edification from Last Wills and Testaments

1. The preamble to Shakespeare's last will and testament was finalized and signed a month before Shakespeare's death in 1616; it is available on public domain websites.

2. The opening and closing paragraphs of Justice Park's last will and testament were published in *The Christian Observer* 38 (1839): 532–33; the person who made the material available is the one who called Mr. Park "a pious layman."

3. Thomas Keayne's last will and testament is so expansive that it is regularly called his *apologia* (defense of his life); it is available online in the proceedings of the December 1954 meeting of the Colonial Society of Massachusetts: https://www.colonialsociety.org.

Devotional 49: All Things Shall Be Well (Julian of Norwich)

1. Julian of Norwich's book came to be titled *Revelations of Divine Love*. For several centuries, it existed in manuscript form only, being first published in 1670. The passage that appears in this anthology is a modernized version of a translation by Grace Warrack published in London by Methuen and Company in 1901. *Revelations of Divine Love* is the first book written in English (actually Middle English) by a woman.

2. Information about T. S. Eliot's role in making Julian of Norwich famous comes from Barbara Newman, "Eliot's Affirmative Way: Julian of Norwich, Charles Williams, and *Little Gidding*," *Modern Philology* 108.3 (2011): 427–61.

Devotional 50: Knowing God (J. I. Packer)

1. The passage is quoted from the twentieth anniversary edition of *Knowing God* (Downers Grove, IL: InterVarsity Press, 1973), 200–1, 228–29. Reprinted with permission of InterVarsity Press (North American rights) and Hodder and Stoughton (original publisher).

2. The claim that Packer wrote so much that it is impossible to compile a complete bibliography is based on the research that the editor of this anthology did when writing a biography of Packer.

Person Index

Scripture Index